Otávio Daros

The Rebellion fan forum and the Britney Spears phenomenon

Otávio Daros

The Rebellion fan forum and the Britney Spears phenomenon

Between consumption and the production of fandom

ScienciaScripts

Imprint

Any brand names and product names mentioned in this book are subject to trademark, brand or patent protection and are trademarks or registered trademarks of their respective holders. The use of brand names, product names, common names, trade names, product descriptions etc. even without a particular marking in this work is in no way to be construed to mean that such names may be regarded as unrestricted in respect of trademark and brand protection legislation and could thus be used by anyone.

Cover image: Provided by the author

This book is a translation from the original published under ISBN 978-3-330-76781-2.

Publisher:
Sciencia Scripts
is a trademark of
Dodo Books Indian Ocean Ltd. and OmniScriptum S.R.L publishing group

120 High Road, East Finchley, London, N2 9ED, United Kingdom
Str. Armeneasca 28/1, office 1, Chisinau MD-2012, Republic of Moldova, Europe
Printed at: see last page
ISBN: 978-620-8-11314-8

I dedicate this research to all my friends, from every part of Brazil, that I have met and
will meet through the forum and Britney.
They are very dear people in my life, who have made me not only laugh out loud, but
also see further.

ACKNOWLEDGMENTS

I am immensely grateful for the serene company of Professor Francisco Rudiger throughout the research process. Thanks to his availability and critical thinking, I was able to develop the work in a way that was enriching for me, which gave me a happy experience as a young researcher. Together with him, I also had the opportunity to come into contact with many thinkers who have contributed to the study of culture and the world of ideas.

I would also like to thank the sociologist Chris Rojek, whose work has broadened my horizons in the study of celebrities and fans.

There was a time in my life when I couldn't leave the house without 20 cars following me. [...] But as time went by, they eased up. They left after I hadn't left the house for two years. [...] It was a bit confusing for me, because I'm a shy person, and I'm not made for this industry because I'm so shy. It's not something I know how to deal with.

Britney Spears, in 2013, after 15 years in the business.

SUMMARY

This paper is a study of celebrity fandom in the context of *internet* discussion forums. The theories presented throughout the research are directly related to the *fandom of* the Brazilian forum *Rebellion,* dedicated to the singer Britney Spears. Firstly, we study the work of Chris Rojek and P. David Marshall, who understand celebrities as cultural fabricators. For the authors, they play important roles in the functioning of modern society, which is marked by the absence of God and the development of the cultural industry. It can be seen that the capitalist system makes exploitative use of star fame. Through them, the business community is able to expand the commercial potential of its products, manufactured by the cultural industry. Up to this stage of the study, fans have been reduced to consumers.

The development of the *internet,* coupled with the emergence of virtual communities and forums, means that people are finding new ways to socialize. Connected by the *internet,* they can communicate even if they are miles apart. In short, social networking *sites* benefit *fandom*'s organization and relationships. Although not intended to liberate them or make them aware of their role as consumers, the organization of *fandom* in virtual spaces encourages fans to develop new skills, such as photo and video editing, and then share them with other members of the *fan base.* On collaborative platforms, such as the *Rebellion* forum, participants can become producers of textual and audiovisual content.

Through links with the work of Henry Jenkins, the research analyzes the form and content produced and shared by the *fandom* that participates in the Brazilian forum.

Keywords: Celebrity; fandom; Britney Spears; forum.

SUMMARY

1 INTRODUCTION

According to Chris Rojek (2008), in modern times celebrities have filled the void left by the Church in society and have served as an instrument for strengthening the cult of distraction, an important pillar of consumer culture. According to him (2008, p. 15), the rise of celebrities can be explained by three major historical processes: the democratization of society, the decline of religion and the commercialization of culture. The progress of mass idols went hand in hand with the expansion of the consumer goods industry and the media, as it was served by it.

In the 21st century, communication faced a paradigm shift. The old logic of traditional media outlets, which were responsible for the entire process of producing and distributing content, has been weakened and now favors audience participation (JENKINS *et al.*, 2014). Technological inventions are benefiting new forms of message production and dissemination, as well as communication and relationships between audiences. Fans of TV, film and music stars also become producers of their own content:

> Audiences are no longer seen as simply a group of consumers of pre-constructed messages, but as people who are shaping, sharing, reconfiguring and remixing media content in ways that could not have been imagined before. And they are doing this not as isolated individuals, but as members of wider communities and networks that allow them to propagate content far beyond their geographical neighborhood (JENKINS *et al.*, 2014, p. 24).

Fandom - a community of fans who share an admiration for the same artist, movie or series - is moving away from the stereotype of a mere group of consumers gathered in a physical or virtual environment to discuss their idols' daily lives and careers. From now on, fans attract attention because they play a more complex role, in that they represent a community that also produces part of what they consume.

For their part, the situation of the stars has changed little. They continue to fulfill practically the same function they were already tasked with: lubricating the consumption of cultural goods and personifying the big brands. Their main role is to stimulate the *fandom* to consume their new products, although ultimately they provoke the group of fans to be more active and participative. As a way of boosting consumption and engaged production, communities and forums, which came about with the flourishing of the *internet,* play a fundamental role in this process, since these *online* spaces organize *fandom.*

Launched in 1998 with the hit song *...Baby One More Time,* American singer Britney Spears is an example of someone who has closely followed the awakening of the *Internet.* According to the *Yahoo!* search engine,[1] Britney is the personality who has topped the list of most searched names on the platform the most times, leading the way in 2005, 2006, 2007 and 2008. She became the best-selling female artist of the 2000s.[2] The public's interest in her led her to tour the United States ten times and launch product lines such as perfumes, dolls, etc. Her growing success and appeal resulted in the creation of thousands of websites, *blogs* and *online* communities, all with the same goal: to gather and organize more fans.

Among the forums listed above is the Brazilian forum *Rebellion,* hosted on the *BritneySpears.com.br* domain. Launched in 2012, *Rebellion* is a virtual space used by the *fandom* to interact and discuss the *pop* singer's life. In 2013, the Brazilian *site* was listed as one of the largest music forums in the world. Since its creation, *Rebellion* has received more than 16,000 registrations.

The preliminary aim of this research is to discover how celebrity culture has developed throughout history. We want to understand, through forum analysis, what are the characteristics and elements of *fandom* formation. By analyzing the *Rebellion forum,* the main objective of the work is to explain the formal and substantial issues of this virtual environment used by fans.

Wasserman and Fraust (1994, p. 10) explain that the analysis of social networks - including discussion forums - is an interdisciplinary endeavor, taking into account studies of social theory, as well as the application of formal mathematics and statistics and computational methods (FRAGOSO *et al.,* 2011, p. 115).

This approach presupposes:

> select the object and form of data collection before starting the analysis. Thus, a first step is to think about how the actors and their connections will be considered, in other words, what will be considered a connection and what will be considered an actor [...] (FRAGOSO *et al.,* 2011, p. 118).

In this case, *Rebellion* is the object of study, the fans registered on the *site* are the actors, and the topics discussed by the members are the connections.

---

[1] http://news.yahoo.com/2013-nostalgic-look-at-yahoo-s-top-10-lists-182809756.html
[2] http://www.chartsinfrance.net/Britney-Spears/news-70558.html

Media celebrities have attracted interest for a long time, as can be seen in the studies of Chris Rojek, set out in the book Celebrity (2008), and in the collection *The Celebrity Culture Reader* (2006), organized by David Marshall. These researchers have contributed to understanding and reflecting on the role of celebrity in the contexts of modern society and the culture industry. Among the articles in Marshall's work, greater attention will be paid to Lawrence Grossberg's text (2006), which relates fanaticism to the psychological field, highlighting aspects such as sensitivity and fantasy.

Through the studies of Henry Jenkins (1992; 2014; 2015), the connection is made between the culture of *fandom* and its organization in virtual communities. To deal specifically with discussion forums, the concepts of Juliano Spyer, a master in digital anthropology, will be used.

In the first chapter of the research, we will talk about the emergence of celebrities and how the rise of the stars was influenced by the decline of the Church and the prosperity of the capitalist system. In relation to the historical context, a distinction will be made between types of celebrity, such as the conferred, who belong to the court and are passed down from one generation to the next; the attributed, who gain *status* through their talent, and come to prominence with the awakening of the theater in England.

Looking closely at the context of capitalism, we discuss the role of mass idols as potential instruments in the social process of the commodification of culture. The usefulness of celebrities in renewing the consumer products of the cultural industry is explored.

In the second section of the first chapter, an attempt is made to understand the role of *fandom*. It is important to emphasize the idea of a group of fans who consume products manufactured by the cultural industry and maintain imaginary relationships with their idols. Then we can understand them as content producers. To conclude the chapter, we present primary concepts about the organization of *fandom* in *Internet* discussion forums.

The second chapter expands on the discussion of forums and looks at *Rebellion* in detail in order to bring it closer to the reader of this monograph. Historical issues related to the emergence of the forum are presented. Formal and substantial aspects of the forum are also presented, such as the number of posts made by fans and information about registered users.

The third chapter serves to deepen the analysis of the forum's content. The main posts - both topics and comments - are specifically analyzed. The most liked posts and those that generated the most debate among forum members are analyzed.

The fourth chapter discusses the bibliography developed in the study and the object of research, in order to articulate the work of the authors and the content produced on the forum. The work of fan artists who have stood out in the *fandom* for the dedication and technical quality of their work is presented here.

The aim of the fifth chapter is to present the production of *fandom* as a form of criticism of the traditional producers themselves, who work for the formal media and are responsible for marketing the products of singers such as Britney Spears herself. Often, the material created by *fandom*, such as music or concert edits, is more creative and of higher quality than the cultural products of the mainstream media. Although this hypothesis does not in any way mean the emancipation of fans or their idols from the industry designed by capitalism.

The research is of the documentary type, since the documentation uses materials that have not yet received analytical treatment. Once this is done, the content check is fundamental to analyzing the form and content of the forum, indicating the relationship between celebrities and their followers. This stage is organized into the following phases: pre-analysis, exploration of the material, analytical treatment of the results and room for interpretation.

It should be noted that the author of this research is responsible for the creation and organization of the forum. Regarding the involvement of the researcher with the object studied, the authors Fragoso, Recuero and Amaral point out:

> The choice of the researcher's degree of inclusion broadens the research options and will imply ethical consequences and even influence the analysis of the research results - in the process of triangulation - and should therefore be properly problematized (FRAGOSO, *et al.*, 2011, p. 194).

The work aims to contribute to the field of social communication insofar as it proposes a reflection on the subject and develops topics that move between cultural studies and cyberculture. The research develops ideas about the relationship between celebrity in the modern context and the cultural industry, as well as the production and consumption of content by fans in the virtual environment, especially in discussion forums.

2 BRITNEY THE CELEBRITY: THE FANS AND THE FORUM

2.1 CELEBRITY

Celebrities are a relatively recent phenomenon. They have been part of society for around 250 years, as British historian Fred Inglis (2012, p. 61) points out. For sociologist Chris Rojek (2008, p. 15), "suffice it to say at this point that the decline of courtly society in the 17th and 18th centuries involved the transfer of cultural capital to men and women who won by their own efforts". Celebrities are modern substitutes for the monarchy, enjoying similar values, such as public recognition, but with a clear distinction: unlike kings and queens, who are sacred figures, they carry the idea of the common man.

Rojek (2008, p. 18) attributes to them the *status of* acquired celebrity and states that their emergence, with actors and actresses on the rise with the theater in England, disputes attention with the conferred celebrities, represented by the monarchy. Until then, the courtly class was sovereign and its authority was hereditary. Therefore, according to Rojek (2008, p. 131), (acquired) celebrities represent the democratization of power in society. This is happening at a time marked by the death of God and an awareness of the meaninglessness of life. When we talk about the end of the divine, we don't mean that society no longer believes in God, but that he no longer occupies the main position in it.

> Religion offers a solution to the problem of structured inequality in this life by promoting eternal salvation for true believers. With the death of God, and the decline of the Church, the sacramental underpinnings of the quest for salvation have been undermined. Celebrity and spectacle fill the void. They contribute to the cult of distraction that values the superficial, the gaudy, the dominance of consumer commodity culture (ROJEK, 2008, p. 99).

It could be said that the cult of distraction and the consumption of merchandise has led to the emergence of a third *status* of celebrity: the attributed. Although they are worthy of success, because they do their utmost to achieve it, their talent is often questioned, since their success is linked to the work of cultural intermediaries: big businessmen and producers.

An example of what can be considered an attributed celebrity is singer Britney

Spears. Her career has been marked by hard work and discipline, from when she was a child dreaming of becoming a dancer and singer, to her success as a teenager. However, like other *pop* singers, Spears' success has been linked to great professionals in the music industry.

Raised in rural Louisiana in the United States, Britney took singing, dancing and gymnastics lessons from her earliest years. Her mother, Lynne Spears, remembers her hard work and dedication:

> When she was two, she danced all over the house, so I decided to enroll her in dance classes to find an outlet for her constant movements. By the age of three, she was the leader of the group. At her first dance recital, her job was to lead all the other little dancers to their positions on stage. During the danpa, all the little girls looked at Britney to make sure they were doing the right steps (SPEARS, 2008, p. 66-67).

In 1993, at the age of 12, Britney joined the cast of the *Mickey Mouse Club,* a classic *Walt Disney* production shown on *ABC*. Little Spears remained on the show until it ended in 1995. She had to return home and, according to Lynne, nothing seemed to shake her dream of singing and dancing professionally. The mother recalls again:

> What's interesting about Britney is that she was always - and I mean always - highly motivated to be the best. She would raise her standards and run after any goal or level of excellence she set her mind to. I never had to tell her to train. Never. In fact, she practiced so much that it drove me crazy (SPEARS, 2009, p. 70).

Unsure which way to go, Britney's family contacted an entertainment lawyer, Larry Rudolph. When Britney turned 15, Rudolph took her to New York to audition for four record labels.

In 1998, Britney signed a temporary contract with *Jive Records*[3] . Rudolph became her manager. Through the intermediary of the label, the singer received from Swedish producer and songwriter Max Martin the song that would become the flagship of her debut album. She released the track *...Baby One More Time* in October of that year and the album of the same title in January 1999, with which she topped hundreds of charts around the world.

Britney's first album sold over 24 million copies worldwide. With this success,

---

[3] The label was dissolved in 2011, transferring its artists to the *RCA Music Group.*

the label contacted Max Martin once again to produce the singer's second album - which went on to sell over 22 million copies[4] . Martin thus became one of the main collaborators in Spears' career. There were more than 12 productions.

In *The Celebrity Culture Reader,* P. David Marshall emphasizes that new stars, such as Britney in the 2000s, represent the vitality of music. The author considers music, more than other cultural products, to be of an irrational order (2006, p. 206). It is strictly linked to emotions and human existence. Realizing this potential of music, the cultural industry, of which the music industry is a part, tries to exploit the public at all costs through the music stars it idolizes.

This means that attributed celebrities, who can be considered cultural fabrications to a certain extent (ROJEK, 2008, p. 12), play a fundamental role in today's society. Today's celebrities, as well as the acquired ones, fill the space that used to be occupied by divine figures and the Church, and provide distraction and entertainment for the masses. And now, in addition, they are part of the machinery that drives the capitalist world and are also responsible for lubricating this great machine, made up of various industries, such as the music industry.

Marshall (2006, p. 197) observes some of the strategies adopted by the industry, such as providing the artist's name next to - and in a similar size to - the title of the song or album on the cover (APPENDIX C). This makes the public immediately relate the work to the singer's name.

The development of the cultural industry has also led to the creation of recording technologies. Marshall (2006, p. 198) explains that this type of resource makes people more concerned about the perfection of the voice. This changes the concept of live performance and how people watch the show. Through music stars, the market has constructed two contradictory levels of the real and the authentic. The recording has become the authentic representation of the music and the concerts the representation of this authentic version. In turn, the concert becomes a ritualized authentication of pleasure and meaning through lived experience, which increases the significance of music and stars (MARSHALL, 2006, p. 202).

This paradigm shift in the music industry implies the emergence and adoption of *playback.* Thus, as Marshall (2006, p. 198) points out, the 20th century was marked by this transformation of the public's experience with music.

Before her stardom, Britney had a powerful voice, with mature, thunderous

---

[4] Available at: <http://www.mediatraffic.de/alltime-album-chart.htm>. Accessed on: 9 Dec. 2015.

vocals for a girl who was just entering her teens. Her mother poetically recalls that Britney would tear the roof off the house singing the latest *hit* by Whitney Houston or Mariah Carey (SPAERS, 2009, p. 70). After being squeezed out of the market, Britney adopted techniques to adapt her voice to *pop* music and make it more commercial. In addition to articulation, Britney positioned her voice in the nasal cavity, which gave - and still gives - her vocals a very youthful look.

As well as technique, Britney had the support of what Marshall referred to above as recording technologies. Spears' changes are noteworthy because to this day they are analyzed by fans and discussed on the *Rebellion* forum.

If, on the one hand, Britney achieved her goal of shaping her voice for the recording studios, on the other, she sacrificed her vocal potential. Lynne regrets the change in her daughter's voice and blames the record company:

> This is coming from the heart of a mother, not a professional record company executive, but before recording studios interfered with that big, strong voice, my sweet girl could tear the roof off a house with her strength and passion. My prayer for Britney, before and now, is that she recovers her real voice, once strong, again, in more ways than one (SPEARS, 2009, p. 102).

To make matters worse, Britney surrendered to the use of *playback,* also mentioned above by Marshall. She became a hostage to it as she provided audiences with fabulous dance numbers, making her performances spectacular, and adapted her voice to the market. *Playback* is the technique of performing by synchronizing lip movements with previously recorded sounds. To this day, Britney can reproduce her perfectly crafted voice in the studio and perform more elaborate choreographies on stage.

For Marshall (2006, p. 196), the growth of *pop* singers is directly linked to the mass reproduction of music, which is due to recording technologies. This creates the music market. Here, the listener is not just a listener, but a potential buyer. By purchasing the music they hear on the radio, the public can feel a sense of ownership over both the music and the artist singing it.

The music industry developed from the youth market that emerged after the Second World War, because, according to Marshall (2006, p. 208), they have been the central point for building stars in recent decades. Teenagers earn their own money. They are paid for the work they do or receive pocket money from family members. But unlike their parents, they don't have as many financial responsibilities, such as paying the rent or other household bills. This way, they can spend their money on leisure activities.

Teenagers have become a valuable target audience for the music industry. To capture this young part of the population, the industry invests in younger stars, as it did in Britney when she was 17 and released ...*Baby One More Time.* Precisely so that fans can identify with their idol. This relationship of identification develops not only through music, but also through style: the way the idol behaves, dresses, looks and speaks.

According to Marshall (2006, p. 208), the music industry sees the *teen* idol as a transitional movement from the toy market, where children are the target audience, to the teen market. They are the cones responsible for preparing the market's new consumers. According to the author, the adolescent idol never appears autonomous: they remain childish and dependent, even after growing up. To this end, the image of the *teen* idol *is* also controlled and worked on by cultural intermediaries to reinforce their limited independence.

As well as singing, Spears' behavior was often directed by commercial agents to build the image closest to the ideal. Being a teenage singer in a country as steeped in Christian values as the United States, meant that Britney had a time and place to inform the press that she was no longer a virgin, for example. The announcement was made in 2003, when she turned 21 (by age in the country), in an interview with W magazine. At the time, part of the media judged Britney as a sinner, for having her first sexual relations before getting married. As a result, Britney's role as the exemplary *teen* idol was broken. There is also the macho attitude of the press, in exempting Justin Timberlake, Spears' ex-boyfriend, from any negative connotation, as a sinner.

In the song *Overprotected,* another Martin production, sung just before she declared her virginity, Britney reveals that she feels overprotected (as the track's title already announces), and how she is controlled by those around her: *I tell 'em what I like / What I want and What I don't / But every time I do I stand corrected*[5] . In another verse, she complains: *I'm so fed up with people telling me to be*[6] .

In 2004, Britney fired her manager Larry Rudolph, who had been with her since her stardom. The decision was seen by fans as an attempt to free the singer, who

---

[5] *I tell them what I like / what I want, what I don't / But every time I do, I'm criticized.*

[6] I'm so tired of people telling me how to be.

seemed tired of following orders imposed by her agents and record label. After four albums and six tours, Britney could take control of her career for the first time - or at least gain more autonomy over it.

Chris Rojek (2008, p. 13) comments that fame causes the subject to disintegrate. The same individual acquires two personalities: the first is the psychic self, and the second is the public face, as others see (or wish to see) the celebrity. In Britney's case, her public self could be a humid country girl, who likes to walk around without make-up, with messy hair and comfortable clothes, as she is photographed to this day on the streets of Los Angeles. Her public self, on the other hand, is impeccable: confident and smiling, with make-up and a dress designed by someone who knows what they're talking about, as she's still photographed doing at the awards ceremonies she attends. This is the Britney that the crowds expect to see when they turn on the television.

"The public presentation of the self is always a staged activity, in which the human actor shows a 'facade' or 'face' to others, while keeping a large part of the self reserved," according to Rojek (2008, p. 13).

The concepts elaborated by Rojek can be problematized when analyzing the author's ideas about the veridical self - the subject while living in the private dimension. Wouldn't contact with any individual represent a loss of the veridical self and benefit the existence of the public self? Living with everyday people, such as family and friends, also represents a threat to the veridical self, since they exert a certain kind of pressure and influence on the subject's behavior. Obviously, fame and crowds tend to expose the subject to much greater tensions, leading them to develop a more ferocious public face. Perhaps the real self that Rojek thinks of only exists when the subject, whether a celebrity or an ordinary person, is isolated.

After distancing herself from her manager, Britney visited a radio station and released the song *Mona Lisa* without the label's permission. The track sounds like a big outburst from the singer. In the verses, she announces her coming decline, which was eagerly awaited by the media and those who had always hoped for her failure: *Now see everyone's watching, as she starts to fall / They want her to break down / And be a legend of a fall*[7] . In another verse, she says: *She's been gone, she's been gone, she's been gone*[8] . In this way, Britney emphasizes the decree of her end.

---

[7] Now look, everyone watching her fall They want her to fail And be the legend of a fall.
[8] She's gone, she's gone, she's gone.

Months later, the label officially released the finished version of the song, but with changes to the lyrics. Instead of singing *She's been gone, she's been gone, she's been gone,* Britney now sings: *Cuz' she's been clone, cuz' she's been clone, cuz' she's been clone*[9] . This could show that the record company wanted to continue investing in Spears' career and that it wasn't over - she still had a lot of records to release and sell.

However, the change in the lyrics of the song suggests another controversial meaning. By saying that it was cloned, many fans understood that Britney was mocking the industry, which was desperately looking for a blonde, sexy young woman who could sing and dance and be able to sell as much as she did at the beginning of her career. At the time, Britney had injured her knee during the recording of the *Outrageous* music video. The singer had to have an operation and, as a result, had to take time off from performing, canceling all her concerts.

Away from the music business, Britney devoted herself to her personal life from 2005 onwards. She got pregnant twice, got married and split up. However, the press also devoted itself to watching and showing the singer's private life with the same intensity. Although the private sphere has been exploited by the media and sold to the public since her emergence, Spears' artistic career has evidently taken a back seat from 2005 onwards. Interest in the singer's life outweighs interest in her work. Music is no longer the biggest business that the industry can extract from Spears. Her life becomes the big business for the celebrity market.

Yahoo! reports that Britney was the most searched person[10] between 2001, 2002, 2003, 2005, 2006, 2007 and 2008 on its search engine. It's worth noting that from 2005 to mid-2007, the singer didn't promote any major musical releases. Even so, she was still the name most searched for by internet users.

The pursuit of dozens of *paparazzi,* the attacks of the tabloid news, added to the crisis in her personal life after her divorce, caused Britney to crumble. In 2007, she was spotted with no underwear on, drunk, shaving her head and hitting a *paparazzo* with an umbrella.

If, at the start of her career, she built up an exemplary image as a professional, sexy, happy and sweet girl, when she freed herself from the commercial agents who

---

[9] Because it was cloned, because it was cloned, because it was cloned.
[10] Available at: <http:llrollingstone.uol.com.brlnoticialbritney-spears-and-one-of-the-most-searched-celebrities-on-site-in-the-last-12-yearsl>. Accessed on: 9 Dec. 2015.

surrounded her, Britney deconstructed this impeccable image. However, she made the decision to manage her own life without learning how to do it first. That had always been the job of her manager and record company.

Regarding her daughter's fall from grace, Lynne asks naively - just as the public and the media have done: "It was Britney, and she was shaving off her beautiful hair. All I could think was: How could that be? She used to be the happiest little girl in the world". (SPAERS, 2008, p. 16)

Taking a closer look, from the very beginning of her career, Britney has shown how paradoxical fame is. In the song *Lucky,* also produced by Max Martin, Britney says: *She's so lucky, she's a star / But she cries, cries, cries in her lonely heart, thinking if there's nothing missing in my life I Then why do these tears come at night?*[11] The song tells the story of a Hollywood girl, at the height of her success, who always presents herself to audiences with a perfect smile (public face). It seems that nothing is missing in her life, because she has achieved everything she wanted, but deep down she feels alone and incomplete (real me).

For Chris Rojek, (p. 161, 2006): "celebrities who are the target of fan wish fulfillment are themselves often the victims of achievement fatigue". According to the author (p. 13, 2006): "The public presentation of the self is always a staged activity, in which the human actor shows a 'façade' or 'face' to others, while keeping much of the self reserved." However, the real self, when it realizes that it is being or has been totally colonized by the public face, can wage an inner struggle with its competitor and make increasingly desperate attempts to regain the position that is itss by human condition.

In the music video for *Hold It Against Me,* another song produced by Max Martin, Britney appears in a battle scene with a second Britney. The two women are identical and try to choke each other. In the end, they both fall together and neither is victorious. In other words, it's not clear which of the two is stronger. Fans understood the scene in the video as an allusion to Britney's struggle as a human being (real self) versus the artist (public face), in a way very similar to what Rojek proposes in his work.

A remarkable paradox of fame is that this desire often culminates either in a feeling of being swallowed up by a public face that is considered alien to the real self, or, worse, in the feeling

---

[11] She's so lucky, she's a star / But she cries, cries, cries in her lonely heart, wondering / If there's nothing missing in my life.

of personal extinction in the eyes of other people who treat the real self as 'not authentic' (ROJEK, 2008, p. 14).

In early January 2008, Spears starred in another episode exposing her ruinous and fragile situation. The singer's mansion was surrounded by six police cars, two ambulances and a fire truck after she refused to hand over her two children to her ex-husband. She was carried on a stretcher to an ambulance. The media turned the case into an event, broadcasting right from a helicopter and chasing her to the hospital. At the end of the same month, Britney collapsed again. This time, the police took steps to block the press.

For Rojek (2008), the self-destruction generated by the celebrity herself, as was the case with Spears, is her last act after no longer recognizing herself. Or what she became after the industry intervened through its cultural intermediaries.

After her latest hospitalization, the Los Angeles Supreme Court placed Britney under the guardianship of her father, Jamie Spears. Months later, manager Larry Rudolph, responsible for the singer's stardom, returned to manage her career. Both remain in these positions to this day. The situation in which the singer finds herself only proves Marshall's thesis (2006, p. 208), concluding that the *teen* idol is worked so hard at the beginning of their career that, even when they become adults, they seem incapable of achieving full independence.

However, the guardianship allowed Britney to regain custody of her children and re-establish her career. Today, the singer has a much quieter schedule of concerts and appearances, which bears no resemblance to her early days of stardom. Much of her time is devoted to her children.

It's interesting to note that after her breakdown, Britney as a public face acquired some of the characteristics of her real self, such as shyness and insecurity. In television interviews, for example, the singer is more reserved about her adolescence. She also appears less concerned than before about her success. This makes it seem as if, after the crises, Britney has lost much of her ambition and has unlearned how to articulate herself as perfectly as she did when she was a *teen* idol.

Like any celebrity, Britney is a cultural fabrication (ROJEK, 2008). She served the industry fiercely for many years, as reported above. She trained to charm crowds with her dance numbers and catchy songs. Such exposure led to her degeneration, and only then did she realize how dangerous fame is. She resumed her career, because the market wanted the singer who sold 100 million records and the fans wanted the girl who captivated them. But the memories of her breakdown and the fear of exposure made Britney seem uncomfortable and inhibited in front of the cameras. It's as if she's unlearned the techniques of the public face. She's denied giving herself body and soul to the industry that made her. Britney is a product, as a celebrity. But unlike in the past, today she is a bad product on the shelf, because she no longer knows how to - or rejects the idea of - selling herself. Resistance from the real me?

The fact is that Britney still demonstrates the ability to arouse curiosity and attraction in her fans. They dream of her and want to have her, through her products - from music to perfumes.

2.2 *FANDOM* CULTURE

The success of a celebrity is determined by its ability to reach the masses, and then involve the subjects who are part of it, in order to be able to arouse a greater feeling in part of them. This is what Marshall previously called affective energy (206, p 212). It partly explains how *fandom* distinguishes itself from other people. The public likes the celebrity, the fandom loves them unconditionally. The public consumes their products, the fan collects their products and buys every single one of them on launch day. The public follows the celebrity through magazines and television, the fan creates or participates in forums and communities exclusively about them.

Etymologically, the word fa is a shortening of fanatic, whose root is in the Latin word *fanaticus*, which, in the literal sense, meant "mad, enthusiastic, inspired by some god", originally "relating to a temple", but soon gained negative connotations: "of people inspired by *orgiastic* rites and passionate frenzy", Oxford Latin Dictionary (JENKINS, 2015).

Jenkins (2015, p. 32) says that "the English abbreviation *fan* first appeared at the end of the 19th century in journalistic reports about those who followed professional sports teams".

However, the author points out:

> As much as the term "fan" was originally proposed in a slightly joking manner and used in a generally sympathetic way by sports journalists, it has never escaped its early connotations of excessive zeal in religion and politics, false beliefs, *orgiastic* excesses, possession and insanity, connotations that seem to be at the heart of the representations of fans that we see in contemporary discourse

(JENKINS, 2015, p. 32).

Rojek (2008) points out that the admiration fans feel for the celebrities they idolize is often condemned in public as an act of false consciousness or slavery to someone who may never know they exist.

> In a more prosaic sense, it falls into the same category of triviality and superficiality. Certainly, relationships between fans and celebrities often involve unusually high levels of non-reciprocal emotional dependence, in which fans project intensely positive feelings onto the celebrity (ROJEK, 2008, p. 57).

Celebrity plays an essential role in today's context. Democratic society has promised that everyone will achieve success through their efforts, since everyone is capable and has merit. However, most people lack personal and professional fulfillment and feel lonely in life, precisely because they don't get the recognition and understanding they want. As a result, Rojek (2008, p. 25) suggests that stars have become an imaginary resource for the fans who idolize them. In the midst of life's difficulties and triumphs, fans turn to them for consolation or to plead for wisdom and happiness, which they often don't find in their surroundings.

According to Rojek (p. 73, 2008), "it doesn't matter that the relationship is basically imaginary, because its effects on the fan's organization of emotions and lifestyle are real". Once the relationship with the idol has real effects, many fans mistakenly believe that the imaginary relationship has the potential to replace relationships with friends, family and work colleagues.

The relationship between fan and idol is built on a paradoxical point: distance. The artist appears on a television channel, while the fan follows him from home, hundreds of kilometers away. The distance prevents the two beings from living together and means that they only see each other in person at scheduled moments, such as concerts, where the artist's public face appears instead of his real self. Distance feeds the fan's imagination by giving them the image that the celebrity has the life of their dreams, in which they are almost a god. By creating this imaginary, the admirer's greatest desire will be to be able to appreciate the person they love so much up close.

To bridge the gap, social networking *sites* are the big bet of the moment, according to the *marketing* teams. *Facebook, Instagram* and *Twitter* are all presented as a means of bringing the ^dols (and the brands) closer to the public. In some cases, the intention is to humanize them, to show what their daily lives are like. In others, the aim is to feed the fabulous aura that has been built up around them by publishing posed and processed photos - correcting imperfections. Although social networks have the potential to bring people together in a virtual way, insofar as they provide the public with a representation of the celebrity, they are no substitute for face-to-face contact, when idol and fan share exactly the same physical space.

In a concert, the artist performs on stage, while the fan watches from the audience, just a few meters away, even if separated by a large gap. This is quite different from the interaction on television, which takes place miles away, for example. However, even the face-to-face experience doesn't escape the capitalist logic of the cultural industry. Knowing about the unconditional love of the fans, the industry exploits them by imposing values much higher than what it spends on the production of the show. Various areas are created that give different views of the concert in order to rank the audience and differentiate the price of tickets. Packages are also invented which include guided tours behind the scenes of the show and autographed gifts such as posters and records, making the price even higher than other tickets. At the exit of the show, it is common for the public to find at least one store with hundreds of products related to the artist. For example, when leaving Britney's resident show space in Las Vegas, fans can even find personalized Christmas ornaments with the singer's border, *It's Britney Bitch,* for 20 dollars.

Since 2010, the *Meet & Greet* has become popular at concerts, *a* moment when fans can get as close as possible to the celebrity and fulfill their dream of having their photo taken with them. This is how the cultural industry commercializes the meeting between fan and idol. On the list of the most expensive *Meet & Greets* is Spears'. The buyer has to shell out 2.5 thousand dollars. Around 20 opportunities are available at each show. The *Meet & Greet* lasts approximately 30 to 60 seconds. There, fans can exchange a few words with the singer, ask for a hug and, at the end, they are invited to the most eagerly awaited part: to take a photograph of the meeting, which they can then show to their friends and, of course, keep as a souvenir.

Music provokes subjective experiences in fans in a unique way, according to Marshall (2006, p. 212). Even if they don't operate identically, the experiences that fans have when listening to a song or attending a concert are correlative to a game of intimacy fantasies. In this way, the relationship between fans and idols is always built on the irrational. This explains why, for example, someone spends $2,500 to spend a few seconds next to an artist. For someone who doesn't share such admiration, the *Meet & Greet* proposal may be absurd and totally irrational, and indeed it is, because the power of a *pop* star is configured around affection, which opposes the rational, and meets what is ludic, magical and emotional.

Marshall (2006, p. 212) argues that the industry's challenge is to keep alive the affective energy that sustains the bond between the admirer and the admired artist. The *pop* star *is* used to capture this energy, especially in the younger audience. If they fail to nurture this affective relationship, the feeling of adoration that their followers share dissipates. This is why it is common for many stars, as they get older, or simply a few years after stardom, to fail to maintain or lose the ability to arouse interest in their fans. When this happens, artists also lose the potential to market and generate new products. In this way, they gradually disappear from the market because, for the cultural industry, they are no longer useful.

For Lawrence Grossberg (2006, p. 582), the fas are incapable of recognizing that the culture they enjoy and idolize so much uses them to exploit them. For example, by taking advantage of the unconditional love they feel to charge them abusive prices, as happens on tours. However, the author proposes a differentiation in the relationship established between fan and consumer. According to him (2006), the consumer's sensibility operates in a more simplified way through the production of momentary pleasure, the power of possession. In this respect, Grossberg (2006) corroborates Marshall's thinking when he says that the sensibility of the fan is different from that of the consumer. In the fan, it operates in the fields of affection and also humor. The sensation of the fa experience is more complex. Affect is capable of providing color, tone or texture, i.e. a less unproductive experience.

In his research, Grossberg (2006, p. 582) divides fas into two segments that dialog with each other. The first comprises the majority of fans and says that they passively consume cultural products. Next, the author talks about a smaller segment of fans who actively interact with culture, adapting cultural products, such as music, in such a way that they are expressions of their lived experiences.

For Grossberg, the active group is a minority. For Jenkins (2015), it is the majority. Although Jenkins' studies (2014; 2015) do not focus on the culture of exploitation that has developed around fandom, as Marshall (2006), Grossberg (2006) and Rojek (2008) accurately denounce. Jenkins contributes to the study of *fandom* by showing his ability to take advantage of this culture and contribute to it generating satisfactory results for him.

Throughout this research, especially in the topics covered by Jenkins, the term *fandom* will be used to describe the group of fans who share admiration for the same cultural phenomenon. The expression comes from the combination of two words of English origin: *fan kingdom* - in Portuguese, reino dos fas.

For Jenkins (2015), fans are not just passive consumers or readers, they are also producers of their own content, who collaborate with their group and the mainstream media. According to the author (2015), *fandom* has become a participatory culture that has transformed the experience of television consumption over the years by producing new material. Today, the same thing is happening - possibly to a greater extent - with the advent of information technology.

Jenkins (p. 56, 2014) believes that "fans have often been innovative in their use of participatory platforms to organize and respond to media texts". Among the participatory platforms is the discussion forum, which has served to organize *fandom* on the internet.

2.3 DISCUSSION FORUMS

In Ancient Rome, the forum was the public square at the heart of a city. In it, citizens gathered to discuss matters of common interest. Many centuries have passed, and the arrival of the internet has given the word a new meaning. Now, a forum is also a virtual space where a certain topic is discussed. If, in Roman times, the big issues to be discussed revolved around politics and religion, in modern society in the 21st century, the hot topics are linked to entertainment culture: soccer, cars, *games* and music.

The forums in question are a 20-year-old phenomenon. They developed from *newsgroups* and electronic mailing lists, according to Spyer (2007, p. 47). The largest forum in the world is the Japanese *2channel*. It publishes more than 2 million messages a day, according to the author. The *site* has achieved such popularity in Japan that its influence has been compared to that of traditional media outlets in the country. Unlike members of Western forums, *2channel* participants are anonymous.

Among the most talked about topics are recipes and *anime-type* drawings.

In the West, music is one of the topics that generates the most forums. In addition to *sites* that bring together fans of hundreds of singers and bands, such as *Digital Spy* in the UK and *Idol Forums* in the US. There are forums dedicated specifically to each *pop* star, usually created by a big fan who wants to host their *fandom* partners. These include *Rebellion* about Britney Spears.

The proliferation of discussion forums on the Internet has given them a series of disparate names. Although they refer to a single model of collaborative platform with few variations, the various names have caused real confusion in the term, as Spyer (2007, p. 46) explains:

> Wall, discussion board, discussion forum, message forum and also the variations that exist in English and are used internationally, such as *web forums, message boards, discussion boards, discussion forums, discussion groups, bulletin boards, talk boards,* fora (plural of *forum)* or simply forums.

For Spyer (2007, p. 46), there is a differentiation between the terms:

> "Mural" - the literal translation of *"bulletin board"* - refers to the common object in schools and colleges, used by the community of students, teachers and administration to communicate with each other by means of written messages stuck on a perforable surface. The *web bulletin board* fulfills this function - group communication - but differs from the physical one in that, as well as disseminating information, it allows the audience to talk to each other through the announcements.

In order to elucidate the discussion, this research focuses on the word forum, as Spyer (2007) does in most of his work, because it is the most well-known term among readers.

The forum is characterized as a platform on which registered users can share information or entertainment content, promote discussions, ask questions of other members or express their opinions through comments. The messages are archived, so the fan is able to read old messages, reply to existing messages and also contribute to the discussion by posting new comments.

On most forums, the visiting user needs to register with the *site*'s system to be able to post messages. In many forums, viewing the discussion folders is also blocked for visitors. Therefore, the only way to access the forum is to register. The registration process involves filling in a basic form which asks for a username, *email address* and password. Next, the user must read the terms of service statement and agree to it.

The final step is to confirm the registration by entering the account verification code received via the *e-mail* address provided in the previous form.

To encourage registration, many forums offer visitors the possibility of registering via social networks. When opting for this alternative, the user must enter the *login* and password of any account they have on *sites* such as *Facebook* or *Twitter*.

It's common for fans to register with a pseudonym or nickname instead of their real name. It's also common for people to use images of celebrities or characters from series or films that they are fans of as their profile picture, instead of using an image that shows their identity. This happens because, at first, the user is not used to it and has no relationship with the other participants in the space. Or because they are afraid of having their real name and identity recorded in unpleasant situations, such as a heated argument.

However, the opposite can also happen. A member can use a fictitious name to provoke fights and disrupt the forum. Chris Rojek (2008, p. 155) warns that transgression is a resource for those who desperately want to attract attention and be noticed in a space.

In order to avoid conflict between members, most forums have a set of rules, which express standards for socializing and using the platform. For example, with regard to the rules of coexistence, users may not use disrespectful words towards other users. And, for example, with regard to the rules of use, users may not submit a signature message with an image larger than a predetermined number of pixels, as this size of image overloads the *site*'s server and hinders the viewing of topics. Failure to comply with the rules may lead to the user being penalized. The penalty will be drawn up and applied by the forum's moderation team.

The moderation team is made up of a group of forum members who are responsible for overseeing the human side (participant relations and conflict resolution) and the technical side (message content and *site* operation). Simply put, if the forum were a city, the moderators would be its authorities.

To strengthen the bond between participants, the moderation team can devise a few strategies: "The agenda can help individuals plan and remember events. The photo gallery serves to encourage the group to form a joint story" (SYPER, 2007, p. 50).

The author adds:

Spyer (2007) compares the dynamics of posting a message on a forum to the process of sending someone an *e-mail*. Both are very similar and simple, with a large text field to fill in. "But instead of this information being transmitted to the mailbox of previously defined people, the discussion on the wall is available to the community of users," points out Spyer (2007, p. 48).

According to him:

According to data taken from *Google Trends,*[12] a tool that shows the popularity of terms and search volume on *Google,* the best-known forum systems are: *phpBB, VBulletin* and *IP.Board* (APPENDIX D).

Launched in 2000, *phpBB* is the most widely used forum management system on the Internet. It is free and open source. The default language of *phpBB* is English, but it has already been translated into several languages, including Portuguese and Spanish. In the same year, *vBulletin* was launched. But unlike *phpBB*, it is paid for. The standard license for *vBulletin 5.0* costs 249 dollars. If the buyer wants the version compatible with access from mobile devices, the price rises to 399 dollars. The advantage is that it has more features than *phpBB*. *IP.Board* entered the market in 2002 as free *software*, but in 2004 it followed the *vBulletin* model.

According to *Google Trends* data analysis, forums have been in decline since 2005. Since then, there has been a migration from these collaborative platforms to social networks.

For Chris Rojek (2008), logging on to a *website* regularly, whether it's a forum or a social network, makes fans create a routine in their own lives, with the aim of

---

[12] Available at: <http://clubetech.com.br/o-fim-dos-foruns-de-discussao/>. Accessed on: Dec. 15, 2015.

filling the void of loneliness caused by the circumstances of today's world. The effect is the same as that of other leisure activities linked to entertainment, such as going to parties or watching soccer matches.

3 *REBELLION:* A FAN FORUM

3.1 HISTORY

Launched on June 30, 2012, *Rebellion* is the result of the merger of two Britney Spears fan forums: *Britney Spears Zone,* commonly referred to as just *Zone,* and *Heaven.* The process of merging and organizing the new forum began in May and ended at the end of June that year. The name of the space was chosen by members of the *site*'s team and refers to the song *Rebellion,* recorded by Britney in 2006. In the song, the singer talks about the feeling of manipulation and attempts at domination articulated by the people she has lived with throughout her stardom: *Be wary of others / The ones closest to you / The poison they feed you / And the voodoo that they do*[13] . In the refrain, she states that rebelling is an act of resistance: *But in rebellion / There's a sparkle of truth*[14] . A snippet of the song was released in 2006 on Britney's official website, and a longer snippet was leaked by fans the following year. However, the full track was never made available to the public. The producer of the recording was Christopher Notes Olsen, who died in 2010 after falling eight stories from a hotel. As a result, the rights to the material are restricted to the RCAIJive *Label Group*, which had no interest in releasing the song because it was composed at a dark time in Britney's career.

The current forum is available at *BritneySpears.com.br* and its collaborative platform has more than 16,000 registered fans, located in all regions of Brazil. In a survey, 46% of fans declared themselves to be from the southeast, 16% from the south, 21% from the northeast, 8% from the north, 5% from the center-west and 3% from another country.[15] In another sample, 57% of fans are men and 43% are women. Among them, 35% are aged between 18 and 24. Of the women, 26% are aged between 18 and 24.[16]

Started on January 29, 2012, *Heaven* was the first discussion forum hosted on

---

[13] Be careful of the others / Those closest to you / With the poison they feed you / And the voodoo they make.

[14] But in rebellion / There is a glimmer of truth.

[15] Available at: <http:Ilwww.britneyspears.com.brIforumItopicl20856-de-onde-voce-el>. Accessed on: 9 Dec. 2015.

[16] Available at: <https:Ilwww.facebook.comIbritneysiteIinsightsI?section=navPeople>. Accessed on: 9 Dec. 2015>. Accessed on: 9 Dec. 2015.

BritneySpears.com.br, which has been providing fans with articles translated into Portuguese about Britney's life and career since 1999. Over the six months it has been active, the forum has had 6.5 thousand registrations. At the time, most members created their profile with the intention of acquiring permission to view the material, not to comment on it or interact with other members. Only around 30 fans made a habit of accessing the forum on a daily basis to make posts and take part in conversations.

With the aim of expanding the forum's participation potential, the *site*'s team sought a partnership with *Zone,* which had a higher number of active fans. Unlike *Heaven,* which was born on the traditional forum model, *Zone* was created as an Orkut community[17] in 2009. At the time, the community had 33,000 members. However, it fell victim to *hackers* and had to be recreated in 2010, when it had 12,000 members. With the decline[18] of Orkut from 2011 onwards, the community's owner, Higor Barbosa, formally acquired a domain[19] on the internet and turned it into a forum.

To keep the forum *online,* Higor relied on the free collaboration of a *webmaster, who* was responsible for managing the visual design and programming part of the *site.* Over the months, the *webmaster* gradually became absent. In May 2012, by coincidence, those responsible for *Heaven* invited Higor to join the two forums. Unable to maintain *Zone,* he accepted.

The forum developed into a stalemate. When they were informed of the merger, many members were in favor of it, but many others condemned the project. Despite the disapproval of a considerable number of people, the site administrators went ahead and launched the new forum. At the premiere, all the fans, even those who were against the idea of joining, created their *Rebellion* accounts and remained active. As proof of this, the first topic on the new forum, which welcomed the *fandom* and provided a tutorial for registration, received 37,744 views and 4,620 comments.

Achievements aside, the following months were marked by friction between members, who split into groups and caused the social disintegration of the forum. In a thread created in December 2012, entitled "The *Rebellion* Farce", member OS[20]

---

[17] The system was created by Orkut Buyukkokten in his spare time, while he was a student at Stanford University and a Google employee, from an embryonic version called Club Nexus, developed in 2001. (RECUERO, 2009 apud HAMPELL, 2004)

[18] *Facebook* and *YouTube* were largely responsible for *Orkut*'s demise, according to a report by Serasa Experian (2013). The social networking site came to an end on September 30, 2014. * The author served as a source for the development of this chapter of the monograph.

[19] *ItsBritneyBitch.com.br,* which is now deactivated.

[20] Othon Silva was studying for a degree in Geography at the Federal University of Rio Grande do Sul. He used to share his scientific articles and philosophical reflections with forum members. Some of his

vented his frustration:

> [...] And yes, I was wrong. I was wrong because Zone and Heaven never ceased to exist. And it would have been much better and easier for everyone if they had never really ceased to exist (cyberspatially speaking). The end of the groups in the unity of a single forum, contrary to what I had concluded, was not a new beginning. [...] In the forum, there were never any ethics, there were never any morals, there was never any peace between the members. Because there was never ONE forum. There has never been one set of members. There are members. There are forums. Putting it all together has led to this. [...] Oh, please! A forum that should, above all, have members who RESPECT Britney Spears, no longer has that. Or at least that's taken a back seat. After all, how many discussions about playback, poorly choreographed routines, poorly chosen outfits, poorly made decisions have we not had here? How many members don't treat Britney Spears like a product, like a Barbie, and when she shows herself to be HUMAN, they don't criticize her, they don't belittle her, they don't abandon her? This is a farce. [...] This is a farce and, after everything I've read here, I've given up on living it. YES, my dears, I admit that I made a mistake when I wrote the article at the time of the forum merger. There's nothing wrong with making mistakes. Making mistakes makes us learn. And I strongly hope that the ERROR that is this forum will turn it into a success, and that Rebellion will exist on its own, and put an end to Zone and Heaven once and for all. Which will be a utopia, if it's up to you (SILVA, 2012)[21] .

Following in the footsteps of OS, some fans have stopped frequenting the forum over time. Others were banned for disrespecting the rules set (APPENDIX A) by the site's moderation team. These included a ban on offensive comments against members of the *fandom* and Britney herself.

Although the creation of *Rebellion* damaged the social bond that existed between the Zone and *Heaven fandom,* since many members of both forums were unable to identify with the new site, the site has increased its number of visitors and gained considerable recognition among the celebrity audience on the Internet.

After completing one year of activity, *Rebellion* has entered the[22] ranking of the biggest music forums in the world, placing eighteenth. The list was organized by the US portal *ATRL* and took into account the total number of posts on each forum. At the time, *Rebellion* had 1.1 million posts.

Rebellion has become a benchmark for releasing exclusive content such as

---

texts are available on his *blog:* <http://geosofias.blogspot.com.br/>. Silva died of cancer in 2014.

[21] SILVA, Othon. Available at: <http://www.britneyspears.com.br/forum/topic/9857-artigo-a-farsa-rebellion/>. Accessed on: 9 Dec. 2015.

[22] Available at: <http://atrl.net/forums/showthread.php?t=382574>. Accessed on: 9 Dec. 2015.

photo shoots, *remixes*[23] , commercials and behind-the-scenes videos. All related to Britney. In 2013, the singer was a judge on the second season of *X Factor,* a music competition program produced by *Fox.* Members of the forum translated and shared the subtitles for each episode with the rest of the fans the day after it aired on US TV. In addition, *Rebellion* has a history of organizing coverage of concerts and events that are on Britney's agenda.

On November 8, 2013, the forum registered its record attendance. The site's counter showed 1,400 *online* readers (both registered and visitors) in the same minute. At the time, the song *Passenger* was leaked, which was part of the singer's eighth studio album, *Britney Jean.* The topic with the audio and lyrics of the track received 3,080 comments and 83,744 views.

3.2 FORM

Discussion forums usually organize their home page in a series of folders. Each one houses a topic. Within each folder, there may be other folders, segmenting the larger theme by subject lines. The topics created by members are published inside these folders, and are sorted by the date of the last post. In this way, the topic at the top of each folder is the one with the most recent post among the topics in that folder.

There are exceptions to this logic. Topics with timeless or very relevant content can be placed at the top of the folder by the moderation team. Even if they receive fewer messages, i.e. are less updated than the others, they will remain at the top of the page.

Rebellion has four main folders on its home page: Britney Spears, General, Support and Team. The first folder - and the main one on the forum - is called Britney Spears. It shares all kinds of content relating to the singer. Inside the folder, there are three smaller folders: Covers, where fan-organized covers of Britney's concerts and events are stored; *Downloads,* where fans share their own productions, which can be videos or *remixes.* It is forbidden to share official Britney songs for *download,* as the

---

[23] Music modified by someone else or by the producer himself.

singer's record label could sue the forum; *Shopping,* where fans exchange and sell materials and collectibles, such as records, books etc. to each other.

Pinned to the top of the Britney Spears folder, there are topics for fans to read summaries of the singer's Las Vegas concert residency since 2013, and to follow the performance of her music videos on *YouTube,* and the sales of her songs and albums on *iTunes, Apple*'s online store.

In the General folder, there are three smaller folders: *Off,* where members talk about other celebrities or discuss topics related to politics, culture, etc.; *Circus,* where fans can chat freely about any topic.

On the attributes of this type of folder, Spyer (2007, p. 49) emphasizes:

> In small communities, which are usually formed to discuss just one subject, there are often folders for free discussion called *off-topic.* These spaces simulate the *happy hour* environments of companies, a place to relax by chatting away, "socializing", talking about the issues of the day, telling jokes and, eventually, opening up new fronts of discussion not foreseen in the original idea.

Completing the General folder: *Blends & Avatars,* where fans display and share their artistic gifts related to image editing. Here, many fans who don't know how to edit commission editing requests from talented fans. They usually fulfill the requests and never charge anything in return. However, Jenkins, Green and Ford (2004) note that when an individual works for "free", they expect some form of (social) payment, which could be in the form of recognition, for example. In the case of the forum, the fan who wins an image edit usually displays it in their signature, below the text of each post. It's similar to an *email* signature, but instead of displaying the phone number or company they work for, fans display these edited images.

In the Support folder, fans are informed of matters concerning the development of the forum and decisions made by the moderation team. Fans can also use the space to report problems and resolve doubts they have about the functioning of the site.

The Team folder is restricted to members of the forum's moderation team. There, administrative matters and *fandom* relations were discussed and evaluated, especially in cases of disagreements between fans. Currently, the team uses a *Facebook* group to discuss these matters.

The moderation of a traditional forum is usually divided into two categories:

administrators and moderators. In addition to these two roles, *Rebellion* has coordinators and *blenders.*

The administrators are the members who own the forum. They have access to all functions and full control of the site. At *Rebellion,* they are: Felipe Cardoso, Higor Barbosa, Otavio Daros and Pedro Calixto.

Moderators have the power to edit the content of topics, transfer topics from one folder to another, notify and ban members for breaking the rules[24] .

Coordinators have a similar function to Moderators. However, they are not given the power to notify and ban members. As soon as the administrators and moderators see that the coordinator has matured, he or she is promoted to the position of moderator. Thus, the coordinator is seen as a primary role, often assigned to new members within the forum organization.

On *Rebellion,* the *blender* role *is* assigned to the user responsible for organizing other members' requests in the *Blends & Avatars* folder. Created in 1995, *Blender* is a tool for creating 3D modeling and animation content. In the forum, *blender is* the guy who masters not only this tool but any other tool capable of image editing. This role is held by member Secretsss. Based on this appropriation of meaning, *blenders* have called their products (edited images) *blends.*

Like Secretsss, the moderators Speed Light, Allhoa and Felipo use a *nickname* to relate to the *fandom* in the virtual environment. In addition to the nickname, it is common for members to use *avatars* (as users' profile pictures are known) of celebrities, singers and actors, instead of a personal photo. The *nickname* and the *avatar* are the first ways that the fan finds to build their identity on the forum.

Speed Light says that he chose his *nickname* from the lyrics of a Britney song, which he likes a lot. The song is titled *Don't Keep Me Waiting* and goes: *Okay, light speed I Turbo, to get to me I Don't play, joke around I One shot, you're killin' me*[25] . The fa says he used the words Light Speed inverted - the correct one would be *Speed of Light* - because it makes the name shorter and more practical. He says he's more comfortable as *Speed* than with his real *name,* because the *nickname* acts as a protection of his intimacy. Since he doesn't feel comfortable with exposure, the nickname allows him to do things he wouldn't do as Matheus.

---

[24] In 2016, eight members act as moderators at *Rebellion:* Fabian Brito, Heline Lemos, Igor Costa, Luciano Mendes, Paola Ribeiro, Speed Light, Allhoa and Felipo.
[25] All right, lightning speed I Turbo, to catch up I Don't get distracted by something I One chance, you're killing me.

> I'm not very comfortable with exposure, so using another name
> is a way for me to protect myself from exposure and allow myself to do
> things that I wouldn't do as Matheus. It's a bit paradoxical because at
> the same time as I use it to avoid exposure, I use it to expose more of
> my personality that I, Matheus, wouldn't expose as Matheus. For
> example, talking about certain racy subjects. I'm not a person who talks
> about sex, for example, openly on *Facebook,* but I could talk about it on
> the forum because I'm protected by *Speed Light.* It's almost an *alter
> ego* (RIVERO, 2015)[26] .

Felipo, who outside the forum goes by FK, says he likes to use his *nickname* so he doesn't have to expose his real name. FK explains: "Sometimes I like the anonymity, especially when I joined the forum and had no idea who was there and how it would work. But nowadays I don't have a problem"[27] . When it comes to his *avatar,* Felipo likes to use photos of artists he likes. Most of the time he selects photos of singers, but eventually he also uses photos of female singers, such as Rihanna and Britney.

3.3 CONTENT

From 2012 to 2015, *Rebellion* recorded more than 2.5 million posts (APPENDIX B) sent by members. The months in which the forum reached the highest number of posts were September 2012 (183,000 messages), January 2013 (141,000) and November 2013 (123,000). The dates when the *fandom* was most active were also the times when Britney was most active in the music market. In September 2012, the singer made her debut as a judge on the *X Factor* in the United States. In January 2013, Britney's song *Scream And Shout* topped the *Global Chart,* which measures the success of songs around the world. In November 2013, she released her new album, *Britney Jean.*

The months with the fewest posts were October and November 2014 (both with 22,000 messages), and June 2015 (20,000). The singer didn't make any major announcements during this period.

Below each post, *Rebellion* provides a "like" option. By clicking on it, the fan shows that they have liked the message sent by the member. Among the most liked

---

[26] RIVERO, Matheus. Interview with Otavio Daros. Porto Alegre, December 4, 2015. The full interview is transcribed in Appendix A of this monograph.

[27] KICHIRO, Felipe. Interview with Otavio Daros. Porto Alegre, December 4, 2015. The full interview is transcribed in Appendix B of this monograph.

posts are the coverage of Britney's concerts in Las Vegas, and reports from fans who have traveled to the city to see the show.

In the coverage threads, it's common for fans to post photos and videos of Britney's performances on the night of the concert. They comment on whether they like the singer's outfit, whether they think she's animated or pretty, for example. Fans on the forum often find these photos and videos on social media profiles such as *Facebook* and *Instagram,* where fans who were present at the concert share their memories of the show.

In the report threads, fans who have been to the shows, or who have met Spears, share their experiences with the *fandom.* The messages in the stories are usually positive and serve as an incentive for other fans to travel to Las Vegas and attend the concerts. In them, the fans narrate from the moment they arrive in the city until the end of the show, when they often see the dancers, assistants and managers who work for Britney.

The most active members of the forum are Mari and Outrageous - the *nickname* comes from a song Britney sang in 2004. Mari has 36,000 posts, while Outrageous has 31,000. Mari, 19, is studying electrical engineering in Recife and doesn't work yet. Outrageous, 23, is studying for a master's degree in Communication Theory at Paulista State University (Unesp).

Active since the forum's debut in 2012, Outrageous explains what keeps him coming back to *Rebellion* on a daily basis:

> It's a very cool space that we've seen emerge from the commitment of the fans and that we enrich in our daily lives, it becomes a routine for us to come here and talk to others about Britney or develop other subjects. We create languages, we have a culture of collective intelligence, in which everyone contributes in their own way, we have an organization of power here and we come together from all over Brazil and the world just because we like Britney. I think we end up developing things here that can be used in society in the real world (MILANI, 2015)[28] .

In order to stimulate so much fan participation, the moderation team has devised strategies, such as a *ranking* system that gives members higher *status* as they generate a greater number of posts. For every 100 messages sent, the member is presented with a *blend,* which is displayed below their profile picture. The *blends*

---

[28] MILANI, Leonardo. Interview with Otavio Daros. Porto Alegre, December 4, 2015. The full interview is transcribed in Appendix C of this monograph.

are taken from Spears' music videos and have different degrees of importance. Having a *blend of* an old music video means having fewer posts, i.e. less *status* on the forum, than a fan who has a *blend of* a new music video.

Another tactic adopted by the moderation team is the *R-Shop.* It works like a virtual store within the forum. The *site*'s system recognizes the members with the most posts and awards them amounts of virtual money. The amount received also varies according to the folder to which the member has posted. The Britney Spears folder is considered the most important and therefore has a higher exchange value than the others. With virtual money, fans can buy fictitious products, such as Spears' albums. These are fictitious products, as they are only symbolic, as they have no functionality other than to give *status* to the buying fan. The *R-Shop* is currently deactivated because its system is not compatible with the new version of the forum *(IP.Board 3.4.6).*

Rebellion virtually reproduced the same principle that drives the capitalist wheel in the real world. The purchasing power of each participant was determined by their productivity (number of posts, in the case of the forum). In turn, the goods acquired were displayed in such a way as to confer power *status* and distinguish their holders from the rest.

4 *REBELLION* SUBFORUMS

4.1 BRITNEY SPEARS SEQUENCE

The topics created in the Britney Spears section are mainly covered by the press, Britney herself, music producers and other celebrities. When the singer visits public or commercial venues, *paparazzi* often take photographs and then send the images to celebrity *websites*. The photos are then posted on the *internet*. Almost as often, the press also publishes news and speculation about Britney, from her new boyfriend to her next album. Fans reproduce the material on the forum to let the rest of the *fandom* know. When Britney posts a personal photo or shares any news about her career on her social networks, the same process of sharing among the *fandom* takes place on the forum.

However, throughout this subchapter, we have chosen to analyze in depth the content of topics in which the role of the fan is that of text producer rather than reproducer. Occasionally, fans publish analyses and reflections on Britney's condition, indicating aspects in which fame (public face) has or has not influenced her personal life (real self). For this purpose, we selected three posts from 2014 and 2015, created by different members.

In the topic "Humility, her name is Britney Spears!", PN says that, although the general public doesn't know it, one of the biggest reasons Britney has so many fans is not her music or her dancing, but her humility and simplicity:

> Today, after so many events in Britney's life and precisely because she is a real person who is not ashamed to show herself to be human, many people already know Britney. Britney Spears is FAR FROM being a futile, snobbish, appearance-conscious person. For many years, she has been accused of being just a pretty face (and body), of not being talented and of living off her image, but would these people be so detached from their own appearance as to completely remove her hair? Hair that very much represents Britney Spears, who doesn't think of a beautiful blonde head of hair when they hear that name? (NAVES, 2015)[31] .

To legitimize his speech, PN stitches his ideas together with quotes from artists and music professionals who knew and worked with Britney. These include stars

---

[31] NAVES, Priscila. Available at: <http://www.britneyspears.com.br/forum/topic/27449-humildade- seu-nome-e-britney-spears/>. Accessed on: 9 Dec. 2015.

Barbara Straisand, Mary J. Blidge, Keri Hilson, Zoë Saldana, director Chris Marrs Piliero and choreographer Brian Friedman. To reinforce her speech, PN clips from interviews in which Britney talks about the little things she loves most in life, such as staying at home to cook and clean, and taking time for herself when she gets out of bed in the morning. The topic is illustrated by images in which the singer appears spontaneous, in ordinary clothes and in everyday activities. In other words, the PN discourse is legitimized.

The topic received 105 replies, nine of which were from PN thanking her for her text. No member disagreed. Half of the comments were simply praising the text. The other half, as well as praising, corroborated the ideas expressed by PN.

JV replied:

> Britney as an artist who inspires the people who gravitate around her (her fans) sends an important message these days: it's possible to reach the top without humiliating others. Quite unlike other pop stars who only got media attention by bad-mouthing Britney. That's what makes her unique: her humanity (VANESSA, 2015)[32] .

GA reveals that the direction the singer's career has taken has left her discouraged as a fan, but remembering what the star has faced and that Britney is still "a very good person" keeps her in the *fandom:* "I don't know if when I get married, have children and so on, I'll still be a fanatic fan, but I'll always have a huge affection for Britney as a person".[33]

In the topic, "The Princess's speech: *then and now"*, HL says: "We always see topics comparing Britney's body, abdomen or aspects of her appearance in general over the years", but "we see few in which we can analyze the changes, or not, in Britney's personality over time, especially taking into account everything that has happened to her".[34]

To do this, HL used eight excerpts from interviews Britney gave at the beginning of her career (between 1999 and 2001) and ten more recent ones (from 2010 to 2015). Her aim was to compare in which situations the singer's discourse remains the same and in which points it has changed over the years.

---

[32] VANESSA, Jane. Available at: <http://www.britneyspears.com.br/forum/topic/27449-humildade-your-name-and-britney-spears/page-2>. Accessed on: 9 Dec. 2015.
[33] ALVES, Gabriela. Available at: <http://www.britneyspears.com.br/forum/topic/27449-humildade- seu-nome-e-britney-spears/page-6>. Accessed on: 9 Dec. 2015.
[34] LEMOS, Heline. Available at: <http://www.britneyspears.com.br/forum/topic/25951-o-discurso-da-princesa-then-and-now/>. Accessed on: 9 Dec. 2015.

In 1999, Spears told *MSN Chat* that when she had children and if they wanted to go into *show business,* she would allow it without any problems. In 2010, after becoming a mother, Britney answered a similar question to *Cosmopolitan* magazine, but the answer was completely different: "I'd lock them in their rooms until they turned 30". In 2001, when asked by *Uol* if she wasn't tired of such a busy life, she replied: "I hate it when I hear celebrities talking about how hard their lives are. [...] I knew from the start what I was getting myself into." In the documentary *I am Britney Jean,* aired in 2013, the singer showed a reverse view of what she said at the time: "It was a bit confusing for me, because I'm a shy person and I'm not made for this industry because I'm so shy. It's not something I know how to deal with".[35]

The topic received 83 comments. In general, the messages were short, between half and two lines, congratulating HL on the idea of the topic. VF evaluated the comparison of the interviews: "It's really interesting to see the change in her maturity. Her current answers are much more concise".[36] While member LN criticized the fact that in one of the interviews, listed by HL, Britney says that in the current phase of her career she's just having fun. "It sounds like she's gotten sloppy about her career and stopped wanting to evolve," argued LN.[37]

In the topic "Britney, the *pop* singer and the 'anti-commercial person'", fans retrieve Britney's speech - "I'm not cut out for this industry because I'm so shy" - and manage to draw distinctions between the real self and the public face present in

Spears.

> She got into the business because she loves being on stage, but being in the media is something different, and she doesn't seem to enjoy it as much. Contradictory? Not so much. Being an artist and being a celebrity are things that usually go together, but they are not synonymous (ARAUJO, 2014)[38] .

The LA member proposes differentiating between the terms artist and celebrity, which are often used synonymously. For him, Spears' passion for singing and dancing since she was a child makes her an artist. The moment she, as an artist, has her work marketed by the industry and is recognized by the media, then she also becomes a

[35] SPAERS, Britney. Available at: <http://www.britneyspears.com.br/forum/topic/25951-o-discurso- da-princesa-then-and-now/>. Accessed on: Dec. 9, 2015.

[36] FARIA, Vitor. Available at: <http://www.britneyspears.com.br/forum/topic/25951-o-discurso-da-princesa-then-and-now/>. Accessed on: 9 Dec. 2015.

[37] NOBRE, Lucas. Available at: <http://www.britneyspears.com.br/forum/topic/25951-o-discurso-da-princesa-then-and-now/page-2>. Accessed on: Dec. 9, 2015.

[38] ARAUJO, Leonardo. Available at: <http://www.britneyspears.com.br/forum/topic/23660-britney-a-cantora-pop-e-a-pessoa-anticomercial/page-3>. Accessed on: Dec. 9, 2015.

celebrity. But, according to him, fame isn't her original goal, it's just a consequence of her will or her talent for the stage.

For DR, the inability to be permanently a public face makes her love Britney:

> And that's why I love this woman so much. I think it's incredible to see her walking down the street with her clothes dirty with paint, with holes in them, her pants dragging, without a bra on and not being "mimimi". Do you want to take pictures? Shoot her, go on! She's not a *Barbie,* she goes to the awards looking beautiful, stunning, but I'm sure that as soon as she gets in the car she'll rip off her earrings, rings, heels and mess up her hair, because she's Britney, she's true to who she is! And that makes me a little fearful about the future... In recent interviews, she's said in no uncertain terms that she's thinking of dropping everything and living in the country with her family, her children and her husband. And I think that's incredible, courageous, befitting the little Louisiana girl we've known for over a decade. It makes me love her even more, but damn it, I don't know if that day will ever come... I dream of her continuing her career, but in whatever way she wants. She's already said that she'd love to go back to making music videos like she used to, just one costume, dancing and that's it. I think that's a good way out. She has to remain true to who she is, and that could mean changes, different paths. I hope she's always close to our eyes, I hope she's always happy (ROCHA, 2014)[39] .

Although DR considers Spears' manifestation of her true self in her desire to leave the industry to be courageous, the fan's desire not to lose sight of her idol takes precedence. DR prefers Britney to seek a solution, such as reducing her artistic output, rather than abandoning her career altogether.

4.2 SEQAO ROOFING

The liveliness of the relationship between the celebrity and the fan presupposes a game in which the celebrity is able to continually provoke expectations in the fan and the fan gradually places expectations in the celebrity. However, when one side fails to respond to the stimulus, which is always greater - especially the celebrity because she is the source of it - the other side feels disappointed, which weakens the relationship.

This back and forth of stimuli and responses maintains the affective energy

---

[39] ROCHA, Debora. Available at: <http://www.britneyspears.com.br/forum/topic/23660-britney-a-cantora-pop-e-a-pessoa-anticomercial/page-1>. Accessed on: Dec. 9, 2015.

(MARSHALL, 2006, p. 208) and drives the *fandom*'s interest in participating in Rebellion, but it has also turned the forum into a stage for revolt. In August 2013, Britney posted a timer on her *website*, announcing news about her career for the following month. Days later, *ABC* reported that the announcement would be made during the television program *Good Morning America*. Commercials for the attraction were shown en masse and said that something big and surprising was about to happen to the singer.

The intense publicity created a lot of expectations among fans. The day before the event, the tabloid *TMZ* reported that Britney would be giving a performance to announce her Las Vegas concert residency, due to begin in December of that year. The *website* revealed that 1,350 people would be flown to a desert location in Nevada at 4am, where a huge structure would be set up. Britney would arrive by helicopter and perform her new song *Work Bitch*. The whole thing would be broadcast on *ABC* from 8am.

The singer hadn't performed on stage for two years, so the atmosphere was one of great anticipation and anxiety for the *fandom*. In the early hours of the morning, before the event began, fans organized a coverage thread on *Rebellion* to follow the live broadcast of the event. "I set the alarm, put notices in my mother's and sister's rooms, asking to be woken up," commented one fan. [40]Others said: "I'm afraid I'll miss the time, everything will happen and I'll miss it."[41] "I've just woken up, I've hardly slept". "Oh, what agony. I'm going to miss my exam if I stay here".[42]

By now the thread had received more than 3,000 replies. Hundreds of fans were following the coverage, waiting for the main moment: the performance. "If there's no performance we'll all sue *Good Morning America* for false advertising," warned one member. [43]

Britney arrived at the venue, took part in the program and announced her concert residency in Las Vegas. However, there was no performance. For fans, the announcement of the new residency was not a surprise, as the media had previously reported it. The event disappointed and outraged the *fandom*:

---

[40]   NOBREGA, Matheus. Available at: <http://www.britneyspears.com.br/forum/topic/16436-cobertura-anuncio-da-residencia-de-shows-em-las-vegas/page-100>. Accessed on: 9 Dec. 2015.
[41]   RICARDO, Joao. Available at: <http://www.britneyspears.com.br/forum/topic/16436-cobertura-anuncio-da-residencia-de-shows-em-las-vegas/page-100>. Accessed on: 9 Dec. 2015.
[42]   MORAES, Vanessa. Available at: <http://www.britneyspears.com.br/forum/topic/16436-cobertura-anuncio-da-residencia-de-shows-em-las-vegas/page-205>. Accessed on: December 9, 2015.
[43]   COELHO, Yuri. Available at: <http://www.britneyspears.com.br/forum/topic/16436-cobertura-anuncio-da-residencia-de-shows-em-las-vegas/page-231>. Accessed on: 9 Dec. 2015.

> [...] They've never confirmed anything, but I think some things
> are very inconsiderate. It's true that Britney is already a legend, but that
> doesn't mean she doesn't need to publicize it. But what annoys me
> most is that she could do this for us. Because we're the ones who
> make her richer and richer, and it's thanks to us that the music bombs,
> because if it wasn't for us, it might not work. I'm disgusted, I wanted a
> performance!" (MISHIMA, 2013)[44] .

TM's message helps us understand why *fandom* attaches such value to performance. When an artist releases a song, it automatically sends the following message to *fandom:* buy it, play it on the radio, watch its music video. After expending their energy to make the song a success, the *fandom* expects the star to recognize their work and reward them in some way. In Britney's case, fans expected the performance as a reward. Not performing shows that she is unconcerned about the commercial performance of her own product, in which her fans have invested energy (and money). Ultimately, they felt betrayed, because after fulfilling their role in the symbolic agreement, Britney didn't do her part, or at least not in the way she should have.

> I'm not really one for demanding more and more from her, but
> there comes a time when it gets tiring, you know? Britney fans are
> always content with the basics, always content with "almost nothing"
> and I really thought that in this era things would be different, that at
> least once in our lives we would be positively surprised. But anyway,
> I'm just sorry about all this (MESQUISTA, 2013)[45] .

At the time, the North American press took the announcement of the concert residency positively. Especially the local media, which had commercial interests, such as increasing tourism. And for Spears, being based in a single city instead of touring the world meant that she would have a quiet period in her life and more time to devote to her children. Despite the positive reception from the media and understanding that the singer was satisfied, part of the *fandom* disapproved of her stay in Las Vegas. The residency goes against the logic of the tour, in which the idol goes to meet the fans. In the residency, the fans have to meet the artist.

I've been a fan of hers for 8 years, but today was the biggest disappointment of my life! I'll never get the chance to see Las Vegas! And there's no performance! Only the people who

[44] MISHIMA, Tiffany. Available at: <http://www.britneyspears.com.br/forum/topic/16436-cobertura-anuncio-da-residencia-de-shows-em-las-vegas/page-331>. Accessed on: Dec. 9, 2015.
[45] MESQUITA, Caio. Available at: <http://www.britneyspears.com.br/forum/topic/16436-cobertura-anuncio-da-residencia-de-shows-em-las-vegas/page-434>. Accessed on: 9 Dec. 2015.

can afford to go to the United States to see her are lucky! (BERTOLIN, 2013)[46] .

GB's comment demonstrates his feeling of exclusion at being deprived of Spears' new project, of which he has been a fan for eight years. Although he didn't stop admiring her, he was disappointed by her attitude. For audiences outside the United States, exclusion is mainly due to financial reasons and then the distance between one country and another.

4.3 SEQAO *OFF*

After the Britney Spears folder, the *Off* section is the most popular on the forum. They are
8.4 thousand topics and 700 thousand replies. The topics with the most comments were related to interviews that the members conducted with each other. Each week a fan was chosen to be interviewed and, over the course of seven days, answered hundreds of questions sent in by the *fandom.* It was an opportunity for the members to introduce themselves and connect. The interviews took place during *Rebellion's* first two years, between 2012 and 2013. After about 30 interviews, the members lost interest, as they probably got bored of the dynamic. The most popular question, present in all the threads analyzed, was:
"What do you think of me?". The question was usually the interviewing member's first post.

The interviewee also used to talk about situations related to his personal life, such as his relationship with his parents:

> My relationship with my parents is like this, when I left home I was 12. So the distance ended up affecting our degree of friendship, you know, but the love never ended. I don't talk to them much, they don't know much about my life, so it's a bit vague for them, you know. As I left home early, I matured early too. They don't recognize me anymore, they still think I'm the same as I was when I was 12. I feel sorry for them that they haven't seen me grow up. But they admire me and are proud of me. I've always been an exemplary son who likes to study. I really admire them as human beings, they have the most

[46] BERTOLIN, Gabriely. Available at: <http://www.britneyspears.com.br/forum/topic/16436-cobertura-anuncio-da-residencia-de-shows-em-las-vegas/page-398>. Accessed on: Dec. 9, 2015.

beautiful virtues (MARINHO, 2012)[47] .

At the time, EM's interview received 6.5 thousand messages. Of all the interviews, the one with the greatest impact was by member Megamix, who registered almost 15,000 posts. Most of the questions were simple to formulate and also received quick answers, as the participant had little time to answer each question.

Currently, most of the topics published in the *Off* section are related to music, with information on *pop* stars' releases and concerts. In addition to Western singers, Korean singers are also of constant interest to members. This is followed by posts with *trailers of* movie premieres and factual news about Brazil and the international scene.

Topics about politics are rare on the forum. The biggest influx was recorded at the time of the 2014 presidential elections. Some members carried out polls to find out how the *fandom* voted. For example, in August, the Datafolha polling institute showed Dilma Rousseff with 36% of the vote, against 21% for Marina Silva, and 20% for Aecio Neves. In the forum, Dilma and Marina were tied with 46% of the vote, and Aecio with 6%.[48]

Unlike in the public sphere, the *fandom*'s main concern wasn't with issues related to the economy, health and education, which the candidates defended, but mainly with human rights issues.

For example, member HB was disgusted to see that Dilma and Marina were tied in the vote, with the latter, according to him, being against important causes for the *gay* community.

> Gays voting for Marina, who is against *gay* marriage and follows a retrograde evangelical ideology. [...] Even worse is voting for Aecio. [...] Anyway, people need to do some research and get informed because voting for Marina and Aecio is almost as bad as voting for Pastor Everaldo (BARBOSA, 2014)[49] .

After reading HB's comment, CB posted videos in which Marina speaks in defense of the secular state. He replied:

---

[47] MARINHO, Ezequiel. Available at: <http://www.britneyspears.com.br/forum/topic/8216-entrevista-ez/page-136>. Accessed on: 9 Dec. 2015.

[48] Available at: <http://www.britneyspears.com.br/forum/topic/24662-marina-tem-21-no-1-turno-e-empata-com-dilma-no-2/page-1>. Accessed on: 17 Dec. 2015.

[49] BARBOSA, Higor. Available at: < http://www.britneyspears.com.br/forum/topic/24662-marina- tem-21-no-1-turno-e-empata-com-dilma-no-2/page-7>. Accessed on: 17 Dec. 2015.

As you said about marriage: she is an evangelical, yes, but she doesn't let that affect her political and social judgment. She's already made it VERY clear that she's in favor of civil unions, she's not in favor of the sacrament in church, as I'm not either, it's a culture and that's that, it would be the same if anyone, for example, joined the maponry. And in this video about the secular state, she makes the separation between the personal and the political very clear. Let's do more research and not spread false polemics around, if you have any that prove this, show me, because I really haven't found it so far, because I could also be spreading things as true that are false (BARBOSA, 2014)[50] .

In another poll, also conducted on the forum, members discussed religion, the death penalty and homosexuality. According to Datafolha, 85% of the Brazilian population believes that belief in God makes people better.

Among the *fandom,* 79% think it doesn't necessarily make people better. In the population, 46% believe that the death penalty is the best solution. Among *fandom,* the figure is similar: 45%. However, when it comes to *gay* rights, the fans are more disparate: 100% believe that homosexuality should be accepted by society, against 68% of society.[51] One fan argued:

Regarding the questions in the topic, nowadays believing in God has made people worse because of growing and alienated Protestantism. There are still people who use religion to do good for themselves and their surroundings, but pastors are destroying values of kindness and understanding, imposing their fundamentalist beliefs on every possible aspect of society. The death penalty is not the best punishment in Brazil, that's a fact. Our justice system cannot be trusted to that extent, many innocent people would die and it would be an opening for political persecution that would lead to the accused being "legally" put to death. As for homosexuality, this is a human rights issue and shouldn't even be debated anymore. But it has to be, since the population is still induced into a profound ignorance, directly linked to the dictator Protestantism mentioned above. In short, sexual orientation is anything but oppositional and must be encouraged and respected as a matter of urgency. With this, even the morality that many defend will be extended to these citizens (PERANSONI, 2013)[52] .

Throughout the thread, no *Rebellion* member has expressed any doubts about

---

[50] BARBOSA, Caio. Available at: < http://www.britneyspears.com.br/forum/topic/24662-marina-tem-21-no-1-turno-e-empata-com-dilma-no-2/page-7>. Accessed on: 17 Dec. 2015.
[51]   Available at: <http://www.britneyspears.com.br/forum/topic/17577-esquerda-ou-direita-para-brasileiros-acreditar-em-deus-torna-a-pessoa-melhor/>. Accessed on: 17 Dec. 2015.
[52]   PERANSONI, Francisco. Available at: <http://www.britneyspears.com.br/forum/topic/17577- left-or-right-for-brazilians-believing-in-god-makes-a-person-better/page-10>. Accessed on: 17 Dec. 2015.

the *gay* issue, unlike in the discussion of other topics.

5 *FANDOM* AS A CONTENT PRODUCER

5.1 *THE X FACTOR*

In May 2012, after months of negotiations, Spears was announced as one of the judges on *The X Factor* in the United States. The musical competition was first created by *Simon Cowell* for British television in 2004. In 2011, the show was given an American edition on the *Fox* channel. After acquiring the rights to the product, the channel became responsible for producing and broadcasting the show.

After a lackluster debut season, executives hired Britney in an attempt to capture the public's attention and thus improve the ratings of future seasons. The singer was paid 15 million dollars to host *XFactor* from May to December 2012.

The press announced Spears' hiring on a massive scale. Partly in a negative way, by questioning Britney's ability to judge musical competitors, given that she is known for using *playback* in her performances (see the first chapter). On the other hand, it aroused the public's curiosity by announcing that one of the biggest names in *pop* music would be judging new artists on a weekly basis.

The opinions of *fandom* were also divided. Fans saw *X Factor* as an opportunity to strengthen Britney's popularity by keeping her in the media. As well as serving on the jury, the judges are called upon to carry out the show's publicity schedule: press conferences and appearances on other TV and radio programs. As a result, fans were aware that the singer was unlikely to release a new album or go on tour during this period. Her musical career would be on hold. Even though they disapproved of Britney's decision, it didn't cause the *fandom* to disunite or to stop creating expectations with each episode she took part in the competition. On the contrary, the *fandom* organized itself to follow the singer's development.

According to Jenkins *et al.* (2014, p. 56), fans have often been innovative in their use of participatory platforms to organize and work with media content. In the case of *Rebellion* in relation to *X Factor,* the forum had to structure a project to translate the episodes. The program is produced in English and some episodes are over 90 minutes long. As a result, the mass of Brazilian fans would not understand or would have difficulty following the narrative of the show.

So that the entire *fandom* could watch and understand the show, forum members with advanced English applied to translate, learn the subtitling technique and then make each episode available for *download* with Portuguese subtitles. About the process, fa AB explains:

> I had never subtitled anything, I didn't know how to do it, so I had to search the internet for a program that would help me do it. It wasn't much of a mystery other than being able to translate American and English expressions into Portuguese that made sense with the style of the program (nothing too formal, for example). When I started subtitling *X Factor,* I stopped being so critical of subtitles that don't exactly match the audio. It's extremely difficult for the translation to match the exact timing of the speech! When the episode was made available for *download,* whoever downloaded it first would split the minutes. We did the subtitles in Portuguese before any were made available in English, which was much more difficult. It was often difficult to understand what was being said, which led us to discuss the lines more and, as a result, the subtitles took a little longer to finish (as our interaction was via forum messages, the other person's response wasn't always so quick). Despite the difficulties we had - making subtitles was something completely new and we didn't have *closed captioning* in English to help - we managed to finish very quickly. We made the subtitles available around 48 hours after the program was shown (BODANESE, 2015)[51] .

The first episodes of the program were subtitled by just three members. From the twelfth episode onwards, new fans joined the project and learned how to insert subtitles and synchronize them with the audio. "We went from three people to seven. Each person was now responsible for [translating and subtitling] 12 minutes of the program," says AB.

According to Jenkins *et al.* (2014, p. 200), fans who just watch provide value to the people who produce multimedia content, expanding the audience and potentially motivating their work. And, in the case of the subtitled *X Factor* videos, this is promotional work, which has not generated any profit for any of the members.

From this perspective, AB tells us:

> We started doing it for the members of the forum and they motivated us to keep going. The use of the subtitles by other people was a consequence. On the forum, members would wait for our subtitles to be posted and praise both the subtitles themselves and our voluntary work so that they could watch the program. Their recognition and gratitude was what made me happy to be using my time - with classes and an internship, my little time at home was spent subtitling *X Factor* - watching the same seconds 3, 5 or 10 times to find the translation that best fit the context of the program. (BODANESE, 2015)

Collaborating with Jenkins *et al.*'s (2014, p. 87) point of view, writers such as

Andrew Keen (2007) suggest that the free work of fas constitutes a serious threat to the long-term viability of content production companies.

Fox aired *X Factor* on September 12 in the United States. In Brazil, the *Sony* channel acquired the rights and aired the show on October 2nd. In other words, the subtitled edition of *X Factor* was broadcast to the Brazilian public almost a month late. *Rebellion* managed to make the subtitled content available two days after the *Fox* broadcast. The collaborative platform made the process much faster than the traditional way. This has led to many Brazilian fans opting to follow the *X Factor* on the forum, instead of watching *it* on *Sony*, which is a pay-TV channel.

5.2 THE CASE OF TURNE *CIRCUS*

The Circus Starring: Britney Spears, or simply the *Circus* tour, was the singer's first world tour since 2004, when she injured her knee and had to step away from the stage. Between March and November 2009, Spears visited three continents - North America, Europe and Oceania - and performed 97 shows, grossing more than 130 million dollars, making it the singer's main tour.[53]

The *Circus* tour symbolized Britney's return to the big stage. After five years, thousands of North American, Canadian, European and Australian fans were once again able to attend one of her concerts. However, countries like Brazil and Mexico, which also have significant numbers of fans, did not host the concerts. There was a great deal of hope from the *fandoms* that at least one of the concerts would be recorded and broadcast on a television channel, or released on DVD.

However, Spears' team never made any information official about the professional recording of the show. In the final stretch of the tour, one of the singer's managers, Adam Leber, warned fans: "Sorry to disappoint you. There are no plans for a *Circus Tour* DVD at the moment. Feel free to send me angry messages wishing me ill".[54]

---

[53] Available at: <https://pt.wikipedia.org/wiki/The_Circus_Starring_Britney_Spears>. Accessed on: Dec. 24, 2015.
[54] Available at: <http://www.britney.com.br/?nid=32805>. Accessed on: Dec. 24, 2015.

In an attempt to replace the official DVD record, several fans got involved in audiovisual projects dedicated to the tour. For Jenkins (2015), initiatives of this kind have the function of solidifying and maintaining fan communities:

> The creation, exhibition and exchange of videos create the conditions for a communal art form that contrasts with the commercial culture from which it derives in its refusal to profit and its desire to share products with others who will value them. *Fan videos* are a source of pride not only for the artists who created them, but also for the *fandom* from which they originated, being a tangible demonstration of the value derived from endless hours gathering tapes and watching episodes. What videos articulate is what fans have in common: shared knowledge, mutual interest, collective fantasies (JENKINS, 2015, p. 250).

fa CL dedicated himself to his *Circus* tour project for four years. He collected and edited over a thousand videos and turned them into a single product. The videos used were recorded amateurishly by other fans who attended the concerts at the time and recorded snippets of the performances. Each night, Spears performed a fixed *set/list of* approximately 18 songs. During the show, the singer moved around three stages. One main stage, inspired by the big circus stages, was connected to two smaller ones. All in 360 degree format.

In other words, no viewer had a front view of Britney throughout the concert. This made CL's editing very difficult, as the videos showed Britney either from the front or from the back. Sometimes close up, sometimes far away, depending on the stage she was on and where the viewer was standing.

CL explains how the project began:

> As a good nostalgia fan, I started watching videos from the beginning of the *tour* and noticed that some were very well positioned and in good quality. And the best thing was when I realized that more fans had posted more videos of the same show from different angles. That got my creative juices flowing and I had to start editing at least one song from the *tour* to see what a professional tour production would look like. Of course, it's difficult with fan videos, but by changing angles you can already notice new things and you realize that you can give it more emotion with your more cinematic, theatrical look, etc. From that first edit, some people asked me to try to do the whole show and I did it little by little and showed it [to the fans], because I was a complete layman when it came to doing the edit in the right programs (LIMA, 2015)[54] .

Jenkins (2015, p. 248-249) analyzes that "most artists entered the field with little technical training and no prior experience, usually having seen someone else's videos at a convention and being inspired to try it themselves", as in the case of Lima, who began by editing Britney's *fan videos*. For Jenkins (2015, p. 241), "fan artists seek a level of technical perfection that is difficult to achieve on home video equipment".

Also according to the author (2015, p. 249), these artists who work with edipao "gain recognition in the national and sometimes international *fandom*" for their work, as happened with CL:

> During the course of the project, I had great *feedback,* not only from people in Brazil, but also from people in the United States, Europe and elsewhere. People who had direct contact with Britney also found out about the project and supported it, because of the whole thing of being a fan doing for other fans, as was the case with Ted Kenney, a producer who took part in the project to record the official DVD of the tour, but which was never recorded because the camera structure wasn't ready in time. These structures were to be used to capture images of the show without disturbing the view of those watching (LIMA, 2015).

CL also explains how the *Rebellion* forum has helped to develop the project over the four years it has been running:

> The forum helped me a lot, it was something I'd been doing since the days of *Orkut,* when the forum was still just an *Orkut* community, and at the beginning I used it to find out what the fans wanted to see most about the tour, the parts they were most excited about, etc. Then, when the forum merged with the *website, I* shared it with old and new people, those who already followed and those who didn't yet know. Apart from the relationship I already had with several people there. The comments, whether good or bad, helped me to reflect more (LIMA, 2015).

Once the show had been edited, *fandom* encouraged Lima to turn the project into a physical DVD. "It was something just for the internet, but as the years went by, more fans began to flock to it and they didn't just want something fictional, they wanted something they could put on their shelves next to Britney's other works," says CL.

However, Jenkins (2015, p. 66) points out: "Few fas make enough money from selling their art to see *fandom* as their main source of income". In CL's case, around 40 DVDs were sold for 55 reais each. He made approximately 600 reais. But, according to Jenkins (2015, p. 66), many earn enough to finance their fandom activities. That is, they turn their art into a cultural product and with the money they receive after the sale, they buy official products sold by the idol's record label, via the cultural industry.

In 2011, after releasing a new album, Britney promoted the *Femme Fatale Tour*. The tour started in June and in August, the *Epix* channel made a professional recording of two concerts in Canada to be shown on television. The material was made into a DVD and sold later that year.

But unlike CL's project, *Epix*'s material has been negatively evaluated by *fandom*. According to reports from *Rebellion* fans, the channel's editing doesn't show Spears' best dancing moments. Instead of focusing on the singer's movements, the camera lens is too wide open, showing the stage from afar or the audience. The members were also annoyed by the audio on the DVD, which they said was not an original recording of the concert.[55]

Fan HE vented: "I cry every time I think about what the DVD would have been like if it had live vocals".[56] While SL complained in another thread: "I think the DVD is fine for a singer just starting out. But a star like Britney deserves a great DVD. Sometimes I don't think her team has Britney-sized noggins".[57]

For Jenkins (2015, p. 102), criticism of professional producers is one of the points that highlights *fandom*. In this case, the fans evaluated the material produced by CL as a good product, while *Epix*'s recording and editing process with professional equipment resulted in a bad product. Unlike CL, the professionals at the television channel didn't have the same sensitivity when it came to capturing the audio and selecting the right angles for the show, as the fans would have liked to see. In other words, unlike CL, the company's product managers didn't work to the *fandom*'s tastes.

---

[55] Available at: < http://www.britneyspears.com.br/forum/topic/11046-dvd-da-femme-fatale-tour-em-3d-received-an-award/page-5>. Accessed on: Dec. 24, 2015.

[56] Available at: <http://www.britneyspears.com.br/forum/topic/12222-vocais-ao-vivo-do-dvd-da-fft-filtered-updated-with-audio-from-3/page-4>. Accessed on: Dec. 24, 2015.

[57] Available at: <http://www.britneyspears.com.br/forum/topic/12011-atualizado-em-entrevista-para-the-rebellion-ted-kenney-talks-about-dvd-dafftour/page-15>. Accessed on: Dec. 24, 2015.

6 CONCLUSION

Britney Spears has thousands of fans in Brazil. Just over 16,000 have registered on *Rebellion*. Today, the forum is numerically the largest community of Brazilian fans of the singer. Of the 16,000 registered members, only a fraction are active: they read and comment on posts. There are even fewer producer members, such as *fan video* editor CL and AB, who translated episodes of the *X Factor* program for the *fandom*. As Grossberg (2006, p. 582) noted, only a minority of fans are active.

What Grossberg can't deny is that participating in forums of this kind provides positive experiences for this minority of fans. For example, CL learned to edit videos to meet a need expressed in the community in which he participated. Fans wanted to see a professional edit of at least one show from *The Circus Starring: Britney Spears* tour. Because, for financial reasons, many were unable to travel to the countries that hosted the show.

At the time, the singer's agents didn't organize themselves to record any of the concerts on DVD or broadcast them on television. As the *fandom* approved and encouraged CL's edits, the fan improved his technique to the point where he sought professionalization and made audiovisual production and editing his future source of income.

Works like CL's also have a critical function. Although Jenkins (2015, p. 280) characterizes it as a playful and subjective critique.

On Spears' next tour, her team mobilized to record and broadcast one of the concerts in Canada. The material was produced and edited by a television channel, but it didn't please the fans. For them, the company ignored the main dancing moments of the concert, which is precisely what CL sought to favor in her editing. CL did this because it knew and listened to the *fandom* that would consume its material. Something that professional editors have not tried to do.

It can be concluded that, in certain situations, fan artists generate cultural products that are closer to the expectations of the *fandom* than paid industry professionals. Unlike the latter, fan artists tend to work on a voluntary basis and aim first and foremost for social recognition by the other members of the group, rather than financial recognition.

We can see that *fandom* production has evolved technically and gained greater visibility, with the democratization of the *internet,* for example. However, fans are still totally exploited, and their suggestions are little heard and do not interfere in the productions released by cultural industry professionals.

Fans pay ever more exorbitant amounts for concert tickets so that they can see their idol in person. At the Las Vegas residency, Spears' followers shelled out 2.5 thousand dollars for a few moments and a photo with the singer. In three continuous years, the show has not been recorded on DVD or broadcast by any channel. The management's strategy is clear: to limit the *fandom*'s access to images of the concert, putting pressure on them to attend the event.

In Brazil, any DVD by an international artist, such as Britney Spears, can be bought for up to 30 reais. For a Brazilian fan to go to the singer's concert in Las Vegas, they will have to spend much more on tickets, airfare and accommodation. This is a business tactic whose main purpose is to exploit *fandom*. This only highlights the fact that fans have very limited power over their idols' artistic decisions. And that the agents of this industry use their fanaticism for profit.

When fans become producers, it becomes clear that the cultural industry's interest lies in promoting products it has already launched and marketed. Not least because, in other cases, the production of *fandom* can run counter to the interests of the traditional means of production and distribution.

During the season in which Spears was a judge on the *X Factor,* the show was available with Portuguese subtitles on *Rebellion* rather than on *Sony, the* channel with the rights to broadcast the show in Brazil. After watching the subtitled episodes on the forum, one wonders if many fans didn't bother to watch the *X Factor* on television. In this sense, *Rebellion* contrasted *Sony*'s interests, since it provided subtitles for the show online earlier than the company did on television. Although the forum's reach is smaller than *Sony*'s, *Rebellion* may have damaged the channel's audience potential.

However, it can be seen that discussion forums are less accessed today than they were five or ten years ago (ANNEX D). The rise of social networking *sites* such as *Facebook has* caused forums to lose visibility and fall into disuse. Looking at the history of visits received by *Rebellion, we* can see some peculiarities. The level of member activity varies mainly according to the movement of Spears' career. When she presents something new, such as a song or an album, the forum registers a high number of visits and posts compared to other times. This shows that the forum is still considered a point of discussion among fans. Perhaps this is because it is a more intimate space, where fans know they will be sharing their views with more like-minded people, than on a *site* as large as *Facebook.*

The members of the forum are homogeneous, aged around 20. It can be seen that the majority are students or professionals who have just entered the market, and that their activity on the forum decreases with the demands of university and work. At almost the same rate, new teenage fans, who have more free time, register on the platform. Thus, there is a renewal of the *fandom* participating in *Rebellion.*

Music, especially *pop* music, *is a* frequent topic of conversation among forum members. They are also fans of other singers, such as Christina Aguilera and Mariah Carey. And they unanimously defend policies and rights for minorities, with an emphasis on LGBT achievements.

It can be seen that fan artists see *Rebellion* as a way of encouraging their work, as it gives them visibility. Many start creating *fan art* after being encouraged to do so by their fellow *fandom* members, and show a preference for posting their *fan art* on *Rebellion* first. They believe that forum members will understand their work better and receive it more positively than people from other *sites.*

Grossberg and Jenkins are unanimous in stating that fans are not simple consumers. Grossberg (2006) states that few of the fans who make up *fandom* elaborate and live aesthetic experiences. Jenkins (2015) argues that *fandom* is made up of many fans who enjoy aesthetic experiences, as it is a common practice of the group to produce meanings through texts and generate content. This research shows that Jenkins' thinking may be mistaken, since a close analysis of the *fandom* participating in the *Rebellion* forum showed that only a minority of fans are active in this process of producing new content.

For Grossberg (2006), everyone has some kind of fanaticism, because no one can live in a world where completely nothing matters. Of course, there are levels of fanaticism and this is a subjective and particular feeling felt by each individual. Being a fan of something or someone presents itself as a new way of dealing with pessimism and frustration in a capitalized and godless world. The forum becomes, to some extent, a refuge as it is seen by the *fandom* as a field of optimism and passion. For Jenkins, *fandom* presents itself as a possibility of escape from this prosaic system, dominated by work. However, as this research points out, *fandom* is trapped in the logic of the cultural industry. It captures the energy of its members and encourages them to work for free to promote idols that it has manufactured itself, in order to produce a new wave of merchandise that will move the market for a period of time to come.

Even acknowledging the relationship between *fandom* and commodified culture, Grossberg emphasizes that the energy expended by fans can have some positive return for them, not reducing fan activity to a mere consumer experience. In this sense, Jenkins' thinking dialogues with Grossberg, when the author says that "*fandom* does not prove that all audiences are active; it proves, however, that not all audiences are passive" (JENKINS, p. 289, 2015). As this research shows, some fans can find learning experiences and pleasure in *fandom*, as happened in the cases mentioned in *Rebellion*.

REFERENCES

FONSECA JUNIOR, Wilson C. **Bibliographical research**. In: DUARTE, Jorge; BARROS, Antonio. Methods and techniques of communication research. Sao Paulo: Editora Atlas, 2006.

FRAGOSO, Suely; RECUERO, Raquel; AMARAL, Adriana. **Research methods for the internet**. Porto Alegre: Sulina, 2011.

GROSSBERG, Lawrence. **Is there a fan in the house? The affective sensibility of fandom.** In: MARSHALL, P. David. The celebrity culture reader. New York: Routledge, 2006.

HELDER, R. R. **Como fazer analise documental**. Porto: University of Algarve, 2006.

HINERMAN, Stephen. **'I'll be here with you': fans, fantasy and the figure of Elvis.** In: MARSHALL, P. David. The celebrity culture reader. New York: Routledge, 2006.

INGLIS, Fred. **A brief history of celebrity**. Rio de Janeiro: Versal Editores, 2012.

LEMOS, Andre. **Cyberculture: technology and social life in contemporary culture**. Porto Alegre: Sulina, 2010.

LEVY, Pierre. **Cyberculture**. Sao Paulo: Editora 34, 2010.

LEWIS, Lisa A. **Adoring Audience: Fan Culture and Popular Media**. New York: Routledge, 1992.

JENKINS, Henry. **'Strangers no more, we sing': filking and the social construction of the science fiction fan community**. In: LEWIS, Lisa A. Adoring audiences: fan culture and popular media. New York: Routledge, 1992.

__. **Convergence Culture**. Sao Paulo: Aleph, 2009.

__. **Invaders of the text: fas and participatory culture**. Nova Iguagu: Marsupial, 2015.

JENKINS, Henry; GREEN, Joshua; FORD, Sam. **Connection culture**. Sao Paulo: Aleph, 2014.

JENSON, Joli. **Fandom as pathology: the consequences of characterization**. In: LEWIS, Lisa A. Adoring audiences: fan culture and popular media. New York: Routledge, 1992.

MARSHALL, P. David. **The meanings of the popular music celebrity: the construction of distinctive authenticity**. In: MARSHALL, P. David. The celebrity culture reader. New York: Routledge, 2006.

__. **Celebrity and power**. Minneapolis: University of Minneapolis Press, 1997.

PRIMO, Alex. **Computer-Mediated Interaction: Communication, Cyberculture,**

Cognition. Porto Alegre: Sulina, 2007.

RECUERO, Raquel. **Social networks on the Internet.** Porto Alegre: Sulina, 2009.

ROJEK, Chris. **Celebrity**. Rio de Janeiro: Rocco, 2008.

RUDIGER, Francisco. ***Theodor Adorno and the critique of the culture industry***. Porto Alegre: EDIPUCRS, 2004.

. **Theories of cyberculture**. Perspectives, issues and authors. Porto Alegre: Sulina, 2011.

SANTAELLA, Lucia. **Cultures and arts of the posthuman: from media culture to cyberculture.** Sao Paulo: Paulus, 2003.

SANTAELLA, Lucia; LEMOS, Renata. **Digital social networks. The connective cognition of Twitter**. Sao Paulo: Paulus, 2010.

SPEARS, Lynne. **Britney Spears: the story behind her success**. Rio de Janeiro: Thomas Nelson Brasil, 2009.

STUMPF, Ida Regina C. **Bibliographical research**. In: DUARTE, Jorge; BARROS, Antonio. Metodos e tecnicas de pesquisa em comunicapao. Sao Paulo: Editora Atlas, 2006.

SYPER, Juliano. Connected: **What the Internet has done to you and what you can do with it**. Sao Paulo: Jorge Zahar, 2007.

APPENDIX

APEN DICE A - Questions answered by Speed Light, moderator of the *Rebellion* forum.

Otavio: Speed Light, what's your real name?

Speed: Matheus Rivero.

Otavio: How did you choose your *nickname?* Do you feel more comfortable using it on the forum?

Speed: So, I chose Speed Light because there's a line from a Britney song that I really like, called *Don't Keep Me Waiting,* which goes *Okay, light speed / Turbo, to get to me / Don't play, joke around / One shot, you're killing me.* I took *Light Speed* and reversed it. The correct one would be *Speed of Light.* But I left Speed Light to make it easier. I'm more comfortable with Speed than with Matheus because it works as a protection for me. I'm not very comfortable with exposure, so using another name is a way for me to protect myself from exposure and allow myself to do things I wouldn't do as Matheus. It's a bit paradoxical because at the same time as I use it to avoid exposure, I use it to expose more of my personality that I, Matheus, wouldn't expose as Matheus. For example, talking about certain racy subjects. I'm not a person who talks about sex, for example, openly on *Facebook,* but I would talk about it without any problems on the forum because I'm protected by Speed Light. It's almost an *alter ego.*

APPENDIX B - Questions answered by Felipo, moderator of the *Rebellion* forum.

Otavio: Felipo, what's your real name?

Felipo: Felipe Kichiro.

Otavio: How did you choose your *nickname?* Do you feel more comfortable using it on the forum?

Felipo: When I was on *Twitter*, my username was Felipzz and I used Felipo as my name. I don't know why, it never really made much sense. But I like it so I don't have to write my real name. Sometimes I enjoy the anonymity, especially when I joined the forum and had no idea who was there and how it would work. But nowadays I don't have a problem. It's even in my forum bio: my *Snapchat* is *FelipeKichiro.*

Otavio: Outrageous, what's your real name?

Outrageous: Leonardo Milani.

Otavio: How did you choose this *nickname?* Do you feel more comfortable on the forum with it?

Outrageous: Because I really like the album *In the Zone* and the song *Outrageous is* on it. Yes, I feel more comfortable not exposing my real name.

Otavio: How old are you? And where do you live?

Outrageous: 23 years old. Ribeirao Preto in Sao Paulo.

Otavio: Are you currently studying or working?

Outrageous: I graduated this year with a degree in Social Communication and I'm now studying on my own. I'm not working. This November I'm trying for a master's degree in communication theory at Unesp in Bauru. My favorite theoretical currents are Cultural Studies, and I'm also very interested in theories like the spiral of silence and agendas.

Otavio: What does the *Rebellion* forum mean to you?

Outrageous: It's a very cool space that we've seen emerge from the commitment of fans and that we enrich in our daily lives, it becomes a routine for us to come here to talk to others about Britney or to develop other subjects. We create languages, we have a culture of collective intelligence, in which everyone contributes in their own way, we have an organization of power here and we come together from all over Brazil and the world just because we like Britney. I think we end up developing things here that can be used in society in the real world.

APPENDIX D - Questions answered by Mari, a member of the *Rebellion* forum.

Otavio: Mari, what's your real name?
Mari: And Mariana.

Otavio: How old are you? And where do you live?
Mari: I'm 19 years old. I'm from Recife in Pernambuco.

Otavio: Are you currently studying or working?
Mari: I study electrical engineering and I don't work.

APPENDIX E - Questions answered by *Rebellion* forum member Andrea Bodanese.

Otavio: What was the process for subtitling the episodes in which Britney took part in the *X Factor?*

Andrea: The *X Factor* subtitles were initially done by me and two other friends. As there were only three of us, we were each responsible for 1/3 of the program. We started subtitling *X Factor*-related material during the interviews. Britney took part in several of them and we realized that many people on the forum didn't understand everything that was being said, so we decided to start subtitling them. As the members liked it, we got together to subtitle the *X Factor* episodes as well. I'd never subtitled anything, I didn't know how it was done, so I had to search the internet for a program that would help me do it. It wasn't much of a mystery except to be able to translate American and English expressions into Portuguese that made sense with the style of the program (nothing too formal, for example). When I started subtitling *X Factor, I* stopped being so critical of subtitles that don't exactly match the audio. It's extremely difficult for the translation to match the exact timing of the speech! When the episode was made available for download, whoever downloaded it first would split the minutes. We did the subtitles in Portuguese before any were made available in English, which was much more difficult. It was often difficult to understand what was being said, which led us to discuss the lines more and, as a result, the subtitles took a little longer to finish (as our interaction was via forum messages, the other person's response wasn't always so quick). Despite the difficulties we had - making subtitles was something completely new and we didn't have *closed captioning* in English to help - we managed to finish very quickly. We made the subtitles available around 48 hours after the program aired. From the 12th episode onwards, more people started taking part in the process, making it much easier. We went from three people to seven! Each person was now responsible for 12 minutes of the program. Although the time each person was responsible for was much shorter, the subtitles didn't get finished as quickly. As there were more of us, not everyone always finished their part at the same time. So we had to wait for everyone to finish, keeping almost the same 48 hours to make it available - but still much faster than waiting for *Sony*'s broadcast or some other team of sites known for making subtitles available.

Otavio: What encourages you to spend your time subtitling for others?

Many people don't know English or, even if they do, they can't understand everything that is said in an interview or on a show. The interviews given before the show aired would certainly not be translated by anyone, which meant that many people were unable to understand what Britney was saying about her expectations/interest in the *X Factor.* So we decided to translate the interviews. We realized that people were interested and that the broadcast on *Sony* would take too long, so we talked about our availability to subtitle the shows as well. Our aim was to make more material available to the forum, helping members and also making it accessible to fans who didn't know about it or didn't usually participate in internet forums. Our subtitles were made available much earlier than those made by any other team. We posted not only on the forum, but also on sites like *Addic7ed,* but always mentioning in the subtitle that we were from *BritneySpears.com.br!* so that the subtitle could be accessed by as many fans as possible. This prompted a team that subtitles a lot of TV shows to contact us, asking if we would be interested in joining the group and subtitling the *X Factor* and the episode of *Glee* that Britney would be taking part in. We declined. Our aim was never to gain recognition beyond the forum. We started doing it for the members of the forum and they motivated us to continue. The use of the subtitles by other people was a consequence. On the forum, members would wait for our subtitles to be posted and praise both the subtitles themselves and our "volunteer work" so that they could watch the program. Their recognition and gratitude was what made me happy to be using my time - with classes and an internship, my little time at home was spent subtitling X Factor - watching the same seconds 3, 5 or 10 times to find the translation that best fit the context of the program.

APPENDIX F - Questions answered by Carlos Lima, a member of the *Rebellion* forum. Otavio: Before you were a Britney fan, did you know how to do the types of music you do today?

Carlos: No. I started out editing Britney and I owe it to her to know as little as I do today, especially because the project lasted four years.

Otavio: How did the project develop?

Carlos: The project started when the tour had already been finalized and until then no official/professional audiovisual material had been confirmed in relation to the tour. As a good nostalgia fan, I started watching videos from the beginning of the *tour* in 2010 and noticed that some of them were very well positioned and of good quality. And the best thing was when I realized that more fans had posted more videos of the same show from different angles, it got my creative juices flowing and I had to start editing at least one song from the *tour* to see what a professional production of the tour would look like. Of course, it's difficult with fan videos, but by changing angles you can already notice new things and realize that you can give it more emotion with your more cinematic, theatrical look, etc. From that first edit, some people asked me to try to do the whole show and I did it little by little and showed them, because I was a complete layman when it came to editing in the right programs. Halfway through, two years into the project, a computer system crash caused me to lose all my files and I had to start all over again. It took me six months to come to terms with the idea that I was going to have to restart work that had already been underway for two years. Two years later, I managed to finish everything, and this time everything worked out. During the course of the project, I had great *feedback,* not only from people in Brazil, but also from people in the United States, Europe and beyond. People who had direct contact with Britney also found out about the project and supported it, for the whole thing of being a fan doing for other fans, as was the case with

Ted Kenney, a producer who took part in the project to record the official DVD of the tour, but which was never recorded because the camera structure wasn't ready in time. These structures were to be used to capture images of the concert without disturbing the view of those watching.

Otavio: How many different videos were used throughout the DVD edition?

Carlos: There were more than a thousand videos. I still have the files... About 1,100 on average.

Otavio: How does the marketing of the DVD work?
Carlos: I buy X amount of DVDs and sell those, then a few months later I buy them again, all because there are so many people and if I left it free for them to buy whenever they wanted, I wouldn't be able to make sure that everyone received a quality DVD at home. The DVD with shipping included cost 55.00. I don't remember the exact amount I sold or the profit, but I sold less than 50 because I set a limit, otherwise it would have been more than 200. My profit didn't reach a thousand, I think about 500 to 600, but I used that to buy more materials.

Otavio: What motivates you to create and share your editions?
Carlos: I really want to work with this, to produce and post-produce a DVD or a record of a show, such as concerts etc., and to do this as a test is very good because as a fan I can have another look at it. There's VBA too, that *fake* movie trailer that people were very supportive of, it was something that came into my head and I needed to share that idea with everyone.

Otavio: Do you sell your work on the forum?
Carlos: Britney's project was something just for the internet, but as the years went by, more fans started to flock to it and they didn't just want something fictional, they wanted something they could put on their shelves next to Britney's other works. That's when they gave me the idea of making a whole case for the DVD and selling it to anyone who wanted to have the physical one.

Otavio: Has YouTube removed any videos from your channel?
Carlos: *YouTube* has never removed any of my Britney-related work, the only thing that's happened is that it's been restricted to certain countries and cell phones. The justification was the copyright on some songs. But I'm not sure about the countries, because *Youtube* has blocked it by region, for example, here in Brazil there are people who can't see it either, but there are also others who can. As for blocking with the cell phone, it has done this as an update to the penalty code when it detects copyright.

Otavio: Was the forum important for the development and dissemination of your work?

Carlos: The forum really helped me, it was something I'd been doing since the days of *Orkut,* when the forum was still just an *Orkut* community, and at the beginning I used it to find out what the fans wanted to see most about the tour, the parts they were most excited about, etc. Then, when the forum merged with the *website, I was* able to share *it* with new and old people, those who already followed it and those who didn't, as well as the relationship I already had with several people there. The comments, whether good or bad, helped me to reflect more. And about editing, yes, I stopped, I started fusing everything in various programs and I kept going through the tutorials until I got to a level where I could mix everything up, do tricks to give a result that the program wouldn't be able to give, you know?

APPENDIX G - Questions answered by Eduardo Morelli, member of the *Rebellion* forum.

Otavio: Before you were a Britney fan, did you know how to do the types of editing you do today? Eduardo: Yes, I did. I'm a graphic designer and illustrator by profession.

Otavio: What motivates you to create and share your editions? Eduardo: Recognition, commitment, love.

Otavio: Do you sell your work on the forum?

Eduardo: Very little. I don't advertise sales. But some of my followers have asked me to create a profile on these *sites* for buying art printed on objects. But, like, I earn 10 reais in a month. The name of the page is *www.society6.com/eduardosmorelli...* There are cushions, t-shirts, mugs, paintings, etc.

Otavio: Have the forum and Britney been important to the development and dissemination of your work?

Eduardo: Absolutely. Britney is an inspiration to me. Her show, her costumes, her concept as a product, all of this I admire, I identify with. Now, the fans are the other half of the orange. They're the ones who like, share and suggest. A large part of my engagement comes from them.

APPENDIX H - Question answered by Heline Lemos, moderator of the *Rebellion* forum.

Otavio: What Britney materials have you leaked to the forum fans?

Heline: There's the *Fantasy Twist* commercial, *a* behind-the-scenes *outtake* from the *Fantasy Twist* commercial, two *outtakes* from *Shape Magazine*, an *outtake from InStyle* and other high-quality photos.

ANNEXES

ANNEX A - **A** set of rules of coexistence given to members by the forum's moderation team. The document was formulated by the moderators in the form of a dialog, in which they answer the main questions of the fans.

Fa comments: Moderapao, frankly, I didn't like the merger of the *Heaven* and *Zone* forums. I hope the merger is undone.

Moderapao replies: *Rebellion* was created for a greater good: to unite us fans. Although we have different histories, we are all the same; we are all fans. And if we're the same, and if we're fans, why can't we share the same space, right? It's never too late to start over, and it's never too late to meet new fans.

Fa comments: I hear the word *flood* a lot, but I don't really know what it is. I think it's forbidden, isn't it?

Moderapao replies: *Flood* means inundation in English. In a forum, a *flood* is an unnecessary post that doesn't add anything to the topic at hand or that goes too far off topic. For example: when a series of posts by the same member are posted in sequence, but none of the posts has any content or opinion; or when members go too far off topic.

Fa comments: What's not to like about members?

Moderapao replies: Don't be disrespectful. There's nothing better than treating them the way you'd like to be treated, is there? Can you play? Of course. Jokes depend on how free you are with them. Oh, and when there's an argument, take a deep breath, try to smooth it over instead of continuing. As Britney used to say: "There's my version, there's your version and there's the truth".

Fa comments: What's not to like about me?

Moderation replies: Perhaps exposing yourself too much. There's no need; it might even sound vulgar. Any pornographic content in itself is not allowed.

Fa comments: And with Britney, if I didn't think that dress was pretty, or I didn't like that haircut, or that choreography of hers, can I talk?
Moderator replies: You can. You have that freedom. The point is not what you say, but how you say it. If you start to be negative about everything, think that nothing is any good, and take offense, thinking that this will solve something, then we feel obliged to intervene.

Fa comments: What about the other artists? Come on, I'm not obliged to like Lady Gaga, Katy Perry, Rihanna, Justin Bieber... But I would like you to like my boys from One Direction.
Moderagao replies: So, let's be fair: no one is obliged to love anyone, and if you make or find funny a joke that says Lady Gaga cross-dresses, for example, you can't think it's wrong for someone to joke about One Direction's sexual orientation.

Fa comments: *Oh my Godney!* So much... I'm afraid of doing something wrong!
Moderator replies: Relax, relax... The intention is to let you know everything. If you slip up, that's fine, we'll talk to you. If you slip again, fine, we'll talk to you... Relax. As moderators, we'll only warn you if we notice that the slips are deliberate, and if you're not showing any interest in correcting them.

ANNEX B - History of the number of messages generated in *Rebellion*.

Month and year	Posts
July 2012	114.362
August 2012	114.574
September 2012	183.004
October 2012	90.840
November 2012	76.691
December 2012	111.133
January 2013	141.451
February 2013	69.578
Margo 2013	43.153
April 2013	43.367
May 2013	45.642
June 2013	39.668
July 2013	51.283
August 2013	42.378
September 2013	101.275
October 2013	79.224
November 2013	123.454
December 2013	112.085
January 2014	52.471
February 2014	49.144
Margo 2014	48.438
April 2014	37.123
May 2014	49.833
June 2014	37.325
July 2014	24.023
August 2014	31.482
September 2014	25.700
October 2014	22.981
November 2014	22.711
December 2014	29.824
January 2015	47.135
February 2015	54.347
Margo 2015	38.505
April 2015	51.824
May 2015	85.701
June 2015	20.275
July 2015	28.069
August 2015	34.399
September 2015	23.037

Source: BritneySpears.com.br

ANNEX C - Example of a cover where the artist's name appears exactly the same size as the album title.

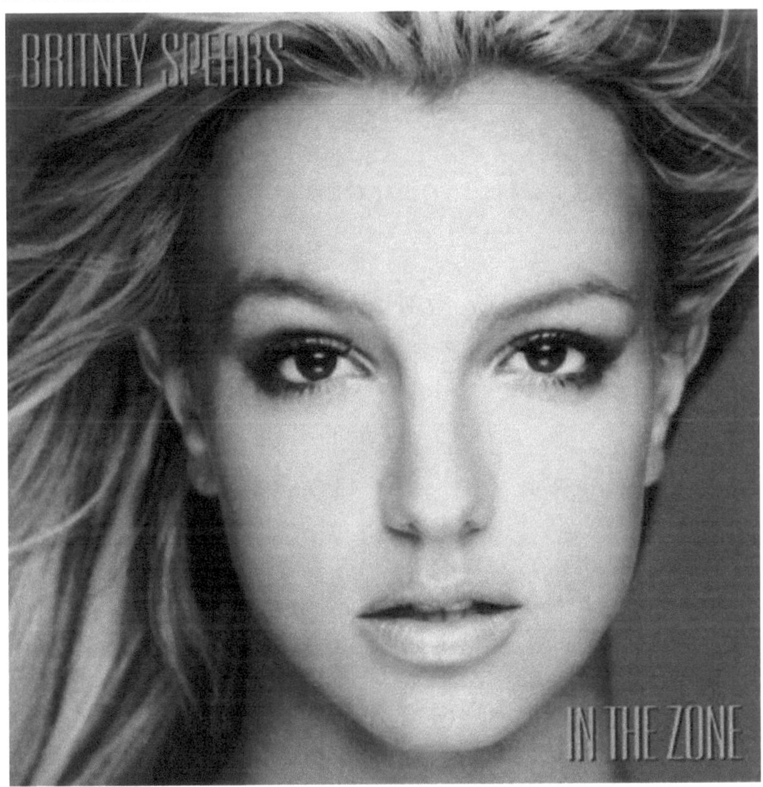

ANNEX D - Graph showing the popularity of forum managers. The illustration is a reproduction from *ClubeTech.com.br*.

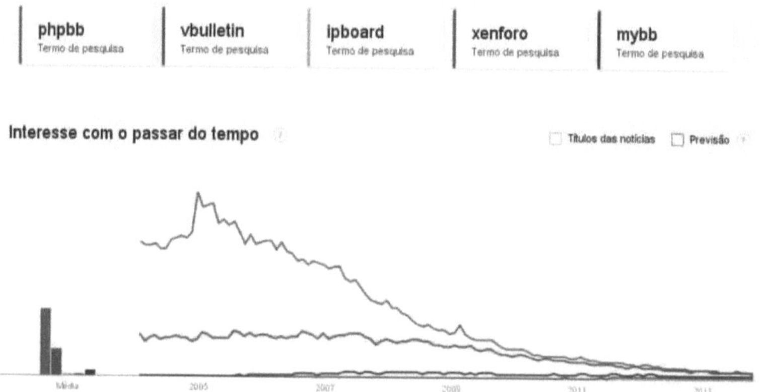

Printed by Books on Demand GmbH, Norderstedt / Germany